# FINDING A HAPPY *Home*

# Endorsements

Jill's memoir offers a look into an exceptional life of resilient trust, obedient faith, steadfast hope, and enduring love. Her life shows what can happen when one says yes to God. Her account not only opens new doors of opportunity, but it also gives hope to countless others who have been marooned in life. Home is a place where you are welcome without having an agenda. Home is a place where you belong. Home is a place where others can find refuge.

Offering a home to children who don't belong or have any other source of refuge is truly ministering to Jesus; so, come along on this journey to read about how God can take the ordinary and transform it into something supernatural. Yes, it will require obedient sacrifice; but the fruit of this obedience will bless generations.

—*Carolyn Ros*
Author, Missionary, Leader at YWAM Amsterdam

Jill and her husband, Paul, became my dear friends when our ministries in Brazil crossed a couple of years ago. What a love and determination I see in this beautiful daughter of God. When you read this story of where she came from, what she has been through, and where she is now, you will be sure nothing is impossible for those who believe! For me, it is an honor to write a recommendation for this inspiring book about overcoming the world with faith. Jill, you are a true inspiration.

—*Brenda Toet*
One in Him Foundation

In fact, there is no greater support than talking about what we live. Sincerity, love, transparency, and a relationship with the Father are what Jill takes with her wherever she goes and wherever God places her. The love and affection she and her husband, Paul, have for our nation is beautiful; and the way God transported them to Brazil is a true miracle, which can only be experienced through faith.

Even though they are foreigners in a nation very different from their own, their courage and boldness are admirable. Through many difficulties, they allowed themselves to experience something completely new by the Lord's leading; and in showing favor to the less favored, they witnessed firsthand a beautiful story of miracles—all by faith, literally. And today, we see just how much God's favor is on their work and on their lives.

If your heart cries out for an intimate experience with the Lord, this book will demand a lot from you! All of the stories that she shares with so much love were lived with great intensity in a life of great communion and surrender to the Lord. I am sure that this reading will take you to a deeper level with God and to a new story in your own life.

*—Joice and Leandro Pasqualeti, Senior Pastors*
Evangelical Community Chamados Church, Holambra, Brazil

We were created to belong, and we were made to be in a family. This has been the mission of Paul and Jill van Opstal Popa—to create a happy home for people who have been left on the outside. In this incredible book, Jill shares their life's journey as they worked with over two thousand children to provide love, care, and hope for their future. They have instilled in these kids the fact that they were created for a reason and that God has an incredible plan for their lives.

You will no doubt laugh and cry as you read their story; but above all, you will find hope in a God Who longs for us to find a happy home in Him.

*—Andrew and Penny Toogood*
Founders and Pastors of Exchange Church, Belfast

It is with great honor that we celebrate the Lar Feliz, an institution that has been a fundamental pillar in supporting and protecting children and adolescents facing social vulnerability. Founded in Jaguariúna on May 2, 2001, by the missionary couple Paul van Opstal, of Dutch origin, and Jill Ann van Opstal, an American, Lar Feliz was established with the aim of sheltering and protecting children and adolescents who, by court order, have been removed from their families due to situations of risk.

Lar Feliz is a non-governmental organization that provides institutional care to children and adolescents in situations of social vulnerability, as outlined in the Statute of the Child and Adolescent (ECA). This care is provided through the protective measures of shelter, in accordance with Article 101 of the ECA. Its mission is to offer a welcoming environment with an adequate physical structure and the necessary support to ensure that these children and adolescents can rebuild their lives safely and with dignity.

Lar Feliz is an example of dedication and commitment to social causes, serving as a pioneer in the Campinas Metropolitan Region and even on a national level, given the complexity of the services offered. They work tirelessly to ensure that every child and adolescent has their fundamental rights guaranteed.

More than just a shelter, the main goal of the Lar Feliz is to re-establish family ties whenever possible, promoting the reintegration of these children and adolescents into their families and communities. To this end, the project works collaboratively with the social assistance network and other organizations in the municipality of Jaguariúna.

Paul and Jill have transformed lives and built dreams over the years. Their dedication not only provides shelter and safety but also offers these children and teenagers the chance for a better future, away from neglect, violence, and abandonment. Lar Feliz is undoubtedly a significant achievement for our city.

Jaguariúna is proud to support and collaborate with this noble initiative. May Lar Feliz continue to be an example of solidarity and social transformation, inspiring our community to always reach out to those who need it most.

—*Gustavo Reis*
Mayor of Jaguariúna

# FINDING A HAPPY *Home*

## A JOURNEY OF FAITH AND REDEMPTION

### JILL VAN OPSTAL-POPA

AMBASSADOR INTERNATIONAL
GREENVILLE, SOUTH CAROLINA & BELFAST, NORTHERN IRELAND
www.ambassador-international.com

# Finding a Happy Home
A Journey of Faith and Redemption, A Memoir

©2025 by Jill van Opstal-Popa
All rights reserved

ISBN: 978-1-64960-691-4, hardcover
ISBN: 978-1-64960-610-5, paperback
eISBN: 978-1-64960-661-7

Cover Design by Karen Slayne
Interior Typesetting by Dentelle Design
Edited by Sara Johnson

No part of this publication may be reproduced, distributed, or transmitted in any form or by any means, including photocopying, recording, or other electronic or mechanical methods, without the prior written permission of the publisher, except in the case of brief quotations embodied in critical reviews and certain other noncommercial uses permitted by copyright law. For permission requests, contact the publisher using the information below.

Scripture taken from the King James Version of the Bible. Public Domain.

This work depicts actual events in the life of the author as truthfully as recollection permits. While all persons and stories within are real, names and identifying characteristics have been changed to respect their privacy.

Ambassador International titles may be purchased in bulk for education, business, fundraising, or sales promotional use. For information, please email sales@emeraldhouse.com.

| AMBASSADOR INTERNATIONAL | AMBASSADOR BOOKS |
|---|---|
| Emerald House | The Mount |
| 411 University Ridge, Suite B14 | 2 Woodstock Link |
| Greenville, SC 29601 | Belfast, BT6 8DD |
| United States | Northern Ireland, United Kingdom |
| www.ambassador-international.com | www.ambassadormedia.co.uk |

*The colophon is a trademark of Ambassador, a Christian publishing company.*

*To the courageous children who came to Lar Feliz—or Happy Home—you are forever in our hearts.*

*To Isa and Jeremy, what a privilege it is being your mom.*

*To Henrique, our Brazilian son, you have given us music.*

*To Paul, my husband, you are my hero. Thank you for loving Jesus with your life.*

*To my mom, Judy, who never doubted that I would become a writer.*

*To our God, Jesus Christ, be all the glory and honor.*

# Table of Contents

Foreword  1
Acknowledgments  3
Timeline of the Places That the van Opstal Family Has Lived  5

Chapter 1
Among Strangers  7

Chapter 2
Without a Home  13
My Grandmother's Secret Recipe  19

Chapter 3
Traveling  21

Chapter 4
Saying Goodbye  27

Chapter 5
Spill the Beans  33

Chapter 6
Home at Last  39

Chapter 7
Lost in the Dark  41

Chapter 8
*A New Day* 53

Chapter 9
*Forming a Dream Team* 57

Chapter 10
*Life Inside of the Home* 61

Chapter 11
*The Blessing of Abraham* 67

Chapter 12
*Stitched Up* 71

Chapter 13
*A Planting* 77

Chapter 14
*The Light at the End of the Tunnel* 81

Chapter 15
*Love Knows No Bounds* 85

Chapter 16
*A New Life* 89

Chapter 17
*Sitting At the Table* 97

Chapter 18
*A Lost Brother and Sister* 103

Chapter 19
*True Love* 109

Chapter 20
*A Dog's Day*   115

Chapter 21
*Child's Play is Divine*   121

Chapter 22
*Walking in the Haunted Wood*   127

Chapter 23
*A Song Sung in the Wilderness*   131

Chapter 24
*The Long Wait*   137

Chapter 25
*Inside Out*   141

Chapter 26
*Home Is Not a Place*   145

Chapter 27
*Under Protest*   149

Chapter 28
*Don't Cry, Baby, Don't Cry!*   155

Chapter 29
*New Places*   161

Chapter 30
*Brother to Brother*   167

Chapter 31
*A Feast*   177

Chapter 32
At Home in Paradise  181

Chapter 33
Shelter or Home  189
Rolled Cookies  193

Chapter 34
It's All a Game  195

Chapter 35
School Break  199

Chapter 36
God is Love  203

Chapter 37
A Tropical Storm  209

Chapter 38
A Day at the Big Tent  215

Chapter 39
Life in the Jungle  217

Chapter 40
Amor  221

Chapter 41
Change of Plans  225

Chapter 42
The Beginning of the End  229

Chapter 44
Light in Their Dwellings  235

Chapter 44
*Almost Home*    241

Chapter 45
*From Death to Life*    247

Chapter 46
*The Last Breath*    253
*Delicious Banana Bread*    256

Chapter 47
*A Double Portion*    257

Chapter 48
*A Beautiful Bride*    261

Chapter 49
*A Ready Bride*    263

Chapter 50
*Back to the Beginning*    265

*Author Biography*    267

# Foreword

Jill van Opstal-Popa is one of the most genuine and pure-of-heart people I have ever met. When you read this beautiful memoir, you will be touched and impacted by her words and her life as they minister to you. This book shares the untold stories of many precious children; and I believe, in some ways, you will hear and see yourself in the accounts shared. Every child deserves a happy home, and every child should be protected and loved. So thank you, Jill and Paul van Opstal, for creating a happy home for God's children.

—Tara McCauley, Assistant Pastor
Rhema Bible Church, South Africa;
Redemption Church, South Africa and the Netherlands;
and founder of Gracious Daughters International

# Acknowledgments

I want to acknowledge all our Brazilian staff from whom we have learned many things, who always strive for excellence and always consider the rights of children first.

I want to thank Jerry Jenkins and the Writers Guild for all the instruction which helped me to improve my craft.

To Ambassador International, I'm so grateful for the opportunity to work with you.

I want to thank Claudia Paoliello Machado de Souza for dedicating her time to translating my first book into Portuguese.

To Ever San Laurenzo, thank you for your beautiful art.

To our families in the USA and the Netherlands, thank you for your love and support.

I want to thank the following churches for all their support and love: Grace Bible Church, De Wijngaard, Barendrecht; Rhema Bible Church, South Africa; Redemption Church, South Africa and the Netherlands; *Comunidade Novo e Livre*; and Exchange Church, Belfast.

To Youth With a Mission, my husband and I are fruits of your work. Keep going strong!

# Timeline of the Places That the van Opstal Family Has Lived

**1990-1996**
Lived in Amsterdam, The Netherlands

**December 20, 1997-February 27, 1998**
On a short-term mission in Sao Paulo, Brazil

**March 1998-November 1998**
Lived in Amsterdam

**November 13, 1998**
Lived in a guest house in Santo Antonio de Posse, Brazil

**Christmas 1998**
Moved to a farm in the neighborhood Guedes

**May 2, 2001**
Opened Lar Feliz at a farm close by Holambra in Jaguariúna

**April 2002**
Moved to Holambra in town

**September 2006**
Purchased our home in Holambra

## CHAPTER 1
# Among Strangers

*"And Jesus said unto him, 'Foxes have holes, and birds of the air have nests; but the Son of man hath not where to lay his head.'"*

Luke 9:58

## Campinas, Brazil
### 1999

Sweat soaked through my husband's polo shirt as he looked at his watch one more time. My face felt as red as wilted tulip petals. I took another swig of the lukewarm water and tried to entertain our two restless toddlers—a girl of four and a two-year-old boy just out of diapers—in the relentless Brazilian heat. With a deck of cards sticky from lollipop fingers, I dealt another hand of Go Fish as we waited at the office of the Policia Federal, hoping and praying to get visas. An older missionary at our church back in Ohio had told me Brazil didn't grant permanent visas anymore. Were we wasting our time here?

A varied group sat outside on that breezeless day, each waiting for their meeting with the police. A stocky woman in a classic polyester suit with dark blonde hair attractively wound into a bun atop her head sat next to us. A few others whispered in Spanish nearby. As strangers, everyone kept to themselves; and none of them attempted to speak English.

Paul, my husband, had gotten us there a full hour ahead of our appointment. I had packed all kinds of essentials to get us through the day. My overloaded vinyl bag included juice, extra clothes, wipes, and games; but I had forgotten sunscreen. The bag stuck to my moist skin like glue.

I decided to try the game I Spy instead of cards. The minutes turned into hours, and time crawled by like a tortoise slowly going out to sea.

"I spy, with my little eye, something black!" I said as two policemen left the building and climbed into their sedan car.

Isa, our daughter, said with a bright smile, "The policeman's gun!" as if she had gotten the answer correct.

"No, the policemen's car!"

A buzz filled the overcrowded place while we waited for news about our visas. It was 11:46, and the bright sun in the clear sky beat down on us. At noon, a brown-eyed, soft-spoken woman wearing a matching blouse and skirt promptly slid the window of the immigration office shut with a loud bang. We were left alone outside the hall with the others, not knowing what to do next or even who we could ask. Paul suggested that the only logical thing to do would be to go out to lunch and come back again when the office opened at 2:00.

We filed down the vintage stairs that were covered in vines and walked half a block to an open restaurant nearby. As was the custom in Brazil, a hot lunch called "almoço" was served in every restaurant in town, the mid meal being the most important of the day. As was our custom, we ordered two dinners with grilled chicken, rice, beans, and salad, with an extra plate of French fries, which was always a good standby for the children. Jeremy, our son, wouldn't even touch a bean. Instead, he ate a plate of white rice with a few pieces of chicken and some hot, crispy fries with a little mayonnaise on the side. Both the children slurped down their guarana, a sweet Brazilian soft drink made from a berry found in the Amazon.

The shaded restaurant on the old side of Campinas was quaintly decorated. Inside was dark because of the smaller windows and large, overgrown trees outside in the garden. It felt considerably cooler; and after the home-cooked meal, we were ready to take on any challenge. Paul paid the cheap bill, took the children by the hand, and walked cheerfully back to the office of the Federal Police. A gentle afternoon rain started coming down, cooling the temperature.

Upon arrival, I noticed a change in the atmosphere. The tension that had been hiding, unseen, in the corners was about to become apparent. As the cleaning lady carefully wiped down the floor with a towel and a squeegee, a lavender fragrance filled the air. Suddenly, I was keenly aware of the sound of ominous whispering. Something bad was about to happen. The window noisily opened, and the friendly clerk kindly asked who was next on the list.

"I am the leader of the group here!" declared a scholarly looking man with glasses covering his narrow eyes. He pulled out a yellowing piece of notepaper from his hip pocket which revealed a list of names written in pen. I could not believe my eyes as we tried to reconcile what was happening and what we would do.

At first, Paul was at a loss for words. Then he asked quietly, "Who put this man in charge? What has given him the right to usurp the authority of the police?"

We realized that while we were gone for lunch, the rest of the group stayed behind and took the opportunity of organizing a list and omitting our family!

The Brazilian woman looked carefully at the paper that was handed to her, then, giving a glance at our direction, said, "I'm sorry! You are not on the list. You will have to return tomorrow!"

"No!" Paul cried. "We cannot return tomorrow!" Walking over to the window, he nervously tried to do something, anything, that would get us an appointment with the visa police that day.

"We have come all the way from Jaguariúna to this city, and our children are so hot and tired! Can't you see how difficult it is?" he asked, pointing his hand toward me and the children who were still trying to grasp what was going on.

The clerk looked over at me as the tears flooded my eyes giving them the appearance of the bright blue Brazilian sky. Both children had reached the limit of waiting and were wiggling in each of my arms. Exhausted and out of ideas, I was unable to keep them entertained for a minute longer. The children were tired and sweaty, sticky, and miserable. They were ready to go back home, as they had missed their naptime.

The clerk hesitated; and suddenly, the crowd began to yell rude things in English, saying that our family had arrived late when we were, in fact, the first ones there. The blonde woman in a polyester suit with a Russian accent started shouting and waving her arms, while a man sitting in the back said among the others, "Poor stupid Americans!"

Even with this going on, it did little to sway the determination of Paul. He was not leaving the police station without an appointment that day, and their outcries had little to no effect on him.

"That list of names is not valid," Paul said very firmly without a care for what the others said or thought. He was Dutch, and his determination served him.

"We will have our moment with the visa police today, one way or another," I said as I looked into Paul's eyes.

The woman studied the list of names, then glanced at me and the children. She crumpled the paper and pushed it to the corner of her desk. "All right, Senhor van Opstal, you may go in and talk with the visa police."

Paul guided me and the children inside before the clerk changed her mind or the others got nasty. We were given our protocol and many forms to fill out, and we received a temporary visa—to our relief. We wouldn't have to go back to the visa police for another year!

For the next five years, we renewed our temporary visas at the Policia Federal. Possibly because of our horrendous first day when the other foreigners had plotted against us, the woman clerk had our faces etched in her memory. A situation that seemed ready to fail, God worked out for good, until one day, there was cause for a celebration!

I called Ohio. "Mom, we have great news! You won't believe it!"

"What is it?"

"We are getting our permanent visas for Brazil!"

"Really? I heard that it wasn't possible to get permanent visas from Brazil! It just goes to show you that all things are possible for God!"

I smiled as I hung up the phone, and that was a day that my faith grew. I had to hang on to that faith because that rocky beginning was only the start of many adventures and mishaps, and the Lord's provision that day would always come back to mind. God must have wanted us here in Brazil. After all, hadn't He parted the Red Sea, making it possible to stay?

As the kids were napping and Paul went to town, I was completely enveloped in loneliness. I was learning to live in an English bubble on the Brazilian countryside. Having been transplanted from the efficient time-oriented land of the Netherlands, our small American-Dutch family had been picked up and placed in a new and wild nation called Brazil. Though the slogan for the nation was "Order and Progress," both were left to be seen or realized at the time that we started our lives there. I had never felt so alone and separated from everything that I loved in life.

## CHAPTER 2
# Without a Home

*"There's no place like home, there's no place like home."*[1]

—Dorothy Gale

I cannot remember, but I have been told that when I watched *The Wizard of Oz* as a little girl, I changed my name to Dorothy and called my brother, Pete, Scarecrow. My brother, Rick, became the Tinman; and my younger brother, Jason, was the Cowardly Lion. Later in life, I ended up far from Kansas, so to speak, in paths that were unknown. I had to make a home in new places far away from my family, far away from Ohio.

As a child, I memorized a story about a bunny looking for a home. Wherever he went, he was unwelcome. He kept searching from place to place for a home until finally he met another bunny who asked him to come in and live.

"'Can I come in?' said the bunny. 'Yes,' said the other bunny. And so, he did. And that was his home."[2]

I learned as a teen girl how precious it was to be welcomed into a new home. It changed everything for me—the path that I was on and my perspective of family. Instead of staying lost, I was found.

---

1  *The Wizard of Oz*, directed by Victor Fleming (1939; Beverly Hills: Metro-Goldwyn-Mayer, 2005), DVD.
2  Margaret Wise Brown, *Home for a Bunny* (New York: Golden Books, 2012).

When I was fifteen years old, my father, Pete, died of what appeared to be an aneurism, leaving my mother, Judy Perry Popa, alone with five children. Tragically, the home I had known was upended; and I found myself wandering, in a sense. After some time passed, my mother became engaged to my stepfather, Lauren E. Baughman, who was himself a widower. The wedding ceremony that followed was held in a small Methodist church where the two families were united. When they wed, we had a combined family of ten. My mom's five—Susie, Pete, Rick, Jason, and myself—and Lauren's three—Larry, Debbie, and Doug—made quite the blended family! Lauren became a father to us all. He did it with a love and ease that is uncommon.

I lived at Lauren's redbrick house in Terrace Hills with the other two teenage children, Doug and Jason. When we moved in, each of us was given our own room.

Lauren told my mom and me, "You can decorate your room any way you want! Buy new carpet and get a new bed—whatever you want to help you feel at home!"

I opted to leave the beautiful hardwood floors in my room and used my mom's Oriental rug, along with a comfortable double bed that was still good as new. I was welcomed in by my stepfather in a warm way, which impacted me for the rest of my life. As a sixteen-year-old, I was sad to leave our Bonnie Lou Drive home; but after moving to Lauren's brick house on Lieb Drive, I felt at peace in a brand-new place.

Even my cat, Catfish, was allowed to stay, though he and Lauren had a strained relationship which began when Lauren agreed to watch him while we were away on vacation. Lauren and the orange cat were never in the same room together; and when Lauren spent the weekend reclining in his chair, Catfish was nowhere to be seen. Perhaps he was in the neighbor's woods, or maybe he was hidden under the barn; but he wouldn't come out until Monday morning when Lauren's truck coasted down the road to work.

Lauren always said, "Catfish can stay, but only because he is Jill's cat. If it weren't for that, he would have to hit the road!" His contagious laugh from his round belly caused everyone else to laugh along with him.

My parents' home would become the base for the adult children to visit, stay for a meal, and talk awhile; so naturally, we needed more room to entertain our very large family. The living room with the cement fireplace and big picture window was too small to hold all the visitors, so Lauren and my mom decided to add a family room. It extended out from the kitchen and ran parallel to the screened-in porch that led to the bountiful garden my mom had planted. It was a cozy room where Lauren spent most of his free time, and we enjoyed football games and old movies on the big screen TV. Those were happy days for our blended family.

Our relatives—the Popas, the Baughmans, and the Perrys—enjoyed many get-togethers over the years, such as Fourth of July parties, hamburgers on the grill, Christmas, and gift exchanges. Everyone was welcome in Lauren's home.

Every Thanksgiving Eve, Lauren was down in the basement working on something at the large pool table. He carefully laid out some kitchen towels, and he had his hands elbow-deep in a bowl of flour. He quietly went to work, kneading the dough into a large ball that he placed on the waxed paper sprinkled with flour. He got out his rolling pin, and he flattened out the dough in a large, rectangular form. Then, taking the smallest butcher knife, he sliced it into noodles to be cooked in the gravy the following day. He always helped my mom by making the homemade noodles; but then he stayed out of the kitchen the rest of the day, parking himself in front of the football games.

Long card tables were set up in a row to fit the whole family at the sit-down dinner. A white tablecloth was placed to make it look like one table, where we would all sit together. Homemade buns; corn casserole; turkey and stuffing; and a plate of pickles and cheeses rounded out the menu, making a huge feast that was more than enough for the big brood of brothers and sisters who would soon come piling in. With shoes stacked at the door, they would stay for the whole day, watching football or playing dominoes or card games until late into the night. Pete, the oldest, would be the last to go home—but not before eating a second helping of pie, turkey, and stuffing. He was always thin, and I wondered where exactly he put all that food!

Lauren had two rules for the household: everyone must make their bed each morning, and we must go to church every Sunday. At the time, I wasn't too sure about those rules, though they were few. At sixteen, I was at the stage in my life that I quietly rebelled, not openly challenging my parents but not completely following them when they weren't around. Weekends were for hanging out with friends who were not the best influence. After attending Lauren's church for some time, I gave my heart completely to Jesus. The old in me became new, and I was able to leave behind my rebellious ways and live a new life by the power of the Holy Spirit and God's grace because of the complete work on the cross by my loving Savior.

After I finished high school, I went to Akron University for a year to study nursing; but I decided to move to Georgia and study world missions at Bible college. This decision meant I had to leave my beloved family behind. Swallowing my fear deeply, I packed up some things and rode the long journey to the Deep South with my parents. With each mile, the distance seemed unbearable. And when we finally arrived at our destination, the three of us formed a circle; and I felt my mother shaking as she cried. At that moment, I realized just how much I was loved by my mom and dad, and I also began to cry tears of joy mingled with sadness. I always thought that no one would ever take the place of my biological dad, Pete, but Lauren did. He was a stepfather who became a father to me.

In all the excitement of the new move to college, I hadn't thought about the separation from my family very much. I was only hoping to fit in with my new classmates and campus life. In this small Bible college in Georgia, I was able to make friends who would be true for a lifetime; and I met my Lord Jesus in a more intimate way while studying His Word. I was so busy that I didn't have time to be homesick, and I didn't realize, until years later, that I left an odd-shaped hole behind at the family table in Ohio. I often wrote letters to my mom and dad to keep in touch. Even though I lived a twelve-hour drive away, we all continued to stay close through letter writing.

People always say that one can never come back home because everything changes and doesn't stay the same. Things would never be the same because I had changed. Still, my mom would have my room just right with a familiar quilt or blanket; and it wouldn't take long before I could rest and enjoy being home, if only for a temporary visit. Even with the many differences of the new places that I lived, I always seemed to find my way back home to Ohio, remembering those favorite places, foods, the fresh country air, and the birds quietly singing in the morning.

Whenever I was home, the family would gather again to eat delicious foods, like ham baked in the oven with fresh buttered buns, hot baked beans, and cream potatoes. A lot can be learned about a family from their recipes, and our family knew the art of planning, cooking, and eating together. Holidays were a priority; and when a date was set to come together, everyone came unless they were deathly ill. There were some index cards, yellowed with time and stains, usually on the counter by the stove with carefully written handwriting. Tried and true recipes, they were carefully guarded for these special occasions. One of these was my sister Debbie's pineapple bread pudding. It was a simple recipe, she said, using only pineapple, a beaten egg, sweetened milk, buttered brown toast, cinnamon, and brown sugar. The smell filled the kitchen.

"Everywhere I get invited to, they always ask me to bring it," said Debbie with a shrug.

Also, coming out of the oven was my mom's delicious baked beans with bacon sizzling on the top. Once I sat down with a filled plate, I tasted the flavors of home and love.

# My Grandmother's Secret Recipe

## Whip Cream Potatoes
Mary Baughman

1. Boil four medium potatoes with the skins left on.
2. Cool, peel, and grate the potatoes.
3. Layer potatoes in an oven dish with salt, pepper, and butter.
4. Pour one half-pint of whipping cream over the potatoes and bake for forty-five minutes at 350 degrees F.

CHAPTER 3
# Traveling

*"What matters remains."*

—Nico Boesten

As an American-Dutch family, we were familiar to traveling. Our kids were accustomed to visiting Ohio in the USA for months at a time. They grew up hearing two different languages and learning about two different cultures. When they were still young, we moved to Brazil, where they learned Portuguese—their third language—and a new, unique culture. They continued to grow like ordinary kids do but with one difference. The world to them was more than just a single place. The world was small enough to discover new places and meet new people who would become friends. We celebrated every Dutch holiday and American holiday, and we would also celebrate every Brazilian holiday. That was a lot of holidays! They continued growing and learning and following Paul and me on our journey.

Furloughs in America were always bittersweet and sometimes challenging. One furlough, as we rode home from a trip to Pennsylvania, I remember being so impressed with the beauty of God while driving through the mountains with the bright sun and the color of the leaves. There were times when I was so tired of traveling—of staying in other people's homes—and I just wanted a home of my own.

# Finding a Happy Home

We were happy in the Netherlands, but soon we would begin a whole different way of life that would leave me longing—at times—for the comforts of Amsterdam.

## Amsterdam, June 18, 1997

*Sunny skies, cool breeze,*
*Bare feet padding along hard wood floors.*
*Pots filled with scented violets;*
*A good cup of coffee.*
*Dutch news,*
*A bountiful, comfy duvet.*
*Welcoming friends.*
*Smiles, encouraging words.*
*A shower like the spring rain;*
*Exercise and walking from place to place.*
*Different types of people,*
*Wearing different types of clothes.*
*Busyness, impatience,*
*Tooting of horns,*
*Bike bells,*
*Longer sunlight hours,*
*Market place,*
*It's good to be home!*

In Amsterdam, we had a large apartment with windows that held a view of the sea. We lived in the center, where it was often noisy at night. Amazingly, the background noise lulled us to sleep. The city streets were filled with people, bikes, buses, and cars. Everything that we needed was close by, so we usually walked everywhere we wanted to go. Outside, the balcony held our container gardens and a sandbox.

Like any ordinary mom, I tended to worry about my kids, Isa and Jeremy, a lot. As always, Paul was more secure, never fearing about what might happen or even what had already happened. I bathed our children in prayers and songs. We played games every day, and we often went to the zoo because we loved to see the animals. Isa was particularly fond of monkeys and bears. Isa also enjoyed playing outside, so there were many days we found ourselves at the park.

Before we moved to Brazil, our family of four traveled with a team of twenty college-age adults to "spy out the land." The first time that I gazed into the face of a little girl living in the slums, I fell in love with Brazil. The seeds of my purpose were planted deep in my heart, which would continue to grow, leaving me discontented until the day when I would return to carry out God's plan. Transition is never easy, and it took so long. Rattling our insecurities, we began pulling up the tent stakes of life in Amsterdam which had been our home for nine years. A new world would be opening soon, and we would see and experience Brazil and live there for the very first time.

*To say goodbye,*
*Not knowing how things will be when I'm not there.*
*To say goodbye,*
*Trusting you in the Father's hands.*
*To say goodbye—*
*Will I ever see your face again?*
*To say goodbye,*
*Going onward like a good soldier on my journey.*
*To say goodbye—*

*Will I ever come this way again?*
*To say goodbye*
*To this lovely place and people.*
*I hope that we will meet again,*
*Maybe one day in the sky.*

Life was a series of hellos and goodbyes. My aunt Jerrie previously taught me how to quilt, so I used that skill as an outlet to cope with the hard transitions. I got out some leftover scraps of cloth and started sewing multi-colored nine-patches, which I joined together with some gray checked gingham cloth. The bright squares in the center reminded me of the beautiful colors of Brazil, and the gray reminded me of the skies during the winters in the Netherlands. I named the quilt "Glory" as a reminder to me of how God joined different types of people for His unique purposes.

My heart started beating faster for Brazil. Our little family would begin the process of packing to make the time-consuming move to a new land. We had to narrow down all our belongings to only eight meager suitcases. We sold the rest of our things for extra money. What we couldn't sell, we gave away. At the time, I didn't consider myself materialistic; but I soon realized in my heart, I treasured a lot of things in our Dutch apartment in the center of Amsterdam. A lot of things that were too big to take along held memories that were precious.

## To Jeremy

*Today I packed*
*Your red boots away,*
*And sadness crept into my heart.*
*Growing up so fast,*
*Our moments together*

*Fleet swiftly by
From the start.*

*There is no denying it—
You're a beautiful boy,
And you grow more handsome every day.
I will always cherish
The touch of your little hands
And your cry for me to come your way.*

*You're a busy boy,
Accomplishing every sort of deed,
Keeping me running to avoid
Catastrophe.*

*The little red boots which were your favorite
Lay empty today.
But I can still see you with them on
Running through the puddles for play.*

*I'm so proud that
You are my little boy.
I'm so happy with you;
These times I will enjoy.*

Philippians 2:3 talks about preferring others above ourselves. Applying that to missions means to respect one another's cultures. When moving to a new country, we learned that there is no such thing as one right way. For the most part, there are two or three different ways to do something right. As a culturally blended family now adapting to the new culture of Brazil, our family customs were usually a mixture of the three—Dutch, American, and Brazilian. I'm thankful for all our travels because Isa and Jeremy gained more holidays and traditions and were richer in their heritage as a result. They grew up loving people from all nations.

## CHAPTER 4
# Saying Goodbye

*"Yea, though I walk through the valley of the shadow of death,
I will fear no evil: for Thou art with me; Thy rod and Thy staff they comfort me."*

Psalm 23:4

## Clinton, Ohio
### 1997

My dad, Lauren, always lay stretched back in his brown recliner to snooze while watching the Colgate golf tournament on the television. He had learned how to play golf when us kids gifted him golf lessons in honor of his retirement. It was a great gift. It was my mom's idea, and it was a winner. It gave him something to look forward to, and it kept him out of the house. The last few months, though, he told us that he hadn't felt like going because he didn't feel like himself, and the dull ache on his side was starting to feel worse.

Lauren was born in 1934 in a small town called Manchester, where he grew up, lived, and would eventually die. It was his home all his days. He was a sickly child when he was growing up, but penicillin had saved his life when he once contracted a bone disease. The doctor told his mother, Mary, that Lauren would have to lose his leg; but just in time, penicillin became available.

My aunt Barb told me how those were dark days for Mary when her husband, Frank, was at war and she was left behind to take care of her four children in their little white house in the center of town. "Laurney," as his sisters had named him, had been sick for a long time. He was finally made well again; and soon after, the news reached them that the war was over. Although typically a quiet family, they celebrated the news by blowing horns and beating on cymbals and drums. Their dad was coming home!

Lauren grew up walking fair, but he was never involved in sports. He was not allowed to join the armed services, though he tried when he was just out of high school. Instead, he served his country as a volunteer fireman for twenty-seven years. Upon finishing high school, he worked driving a backhoe for a construction company called W. G. Lockhart, a family-run business. He was good at what he did and was nicknamed "Captain Crunch." The company originally started out small; but they became unionized, giving the blue-collar worker a good salary and working conditions. Lauren believed in the unions because he saw firsthand how they helped a regular guy have a better life than in the past. He was a member of Ohio Operating Engineers Local 18 since the day it was founded in 1956.

When he was older and working in construction, his leg was crushed by a machine; but he was healed through modern medicine. Later, he was involved in a car accident, which left both of his legs broken. He spent months off work, recovering in his chair and watching sports on the big screen. He finally recovered, but he was not able to return to work; so he retired in 1995.

Lauren was not a material man, but there were a few things in life that he loved: his Ford pick-up truck, his wife and family, his motorbike, and his golf clubs. Being a faithful church-goer, he sat in a familiar pew every week with a blue, leather-bound Bible with his name engraved on the front resting on his lap. He laughed hard at a good joke, his blue eyes twinkling. His favorite meal, which was his signature dish, was macaroni and stewed tomatoes, to which he always added a heaping spoon of sugar; the sweetness balanced out the acidity of the tomatoes. It was a shame that the rest of the family were not fans of the sticky macaroni tomato mixture. I forced it down with a smile, adding some ketchup. Doug liked it, though he always seemed to make plans to go out; and Jason filled up on bread and butter beforehand. It had been a cheap middle-of-the-week meal for all.

My dad suspected, though he didn't quite know, that he was heading into a storm; and the name of it was *cancer*. He was normally quiet and kept everything in, but on this particular day, he called me on the phone, and we both cried. My mom was traveling on a mission trip to Costa Rica, and he was left to deal with the bad test results alone. His adult children were all grown now, living as far away as across the sea to just down the road. This was a path that my dad would walk alone. Though his loved ones were nearby, it was he and his God who would travel this journey through the dark storm ahead.

Paul and I prayed every day that my dad would be healed of cancer. He outlived the prediction of the doctors, but the cancer continued to grow. As his sickness worsened in the months that followed, God began to uproot us from the Netherlands where we were missionaries and to plant us on the mission field of Brazil.

During my last memorable visit with my dad, we laughed and talked, though he was very quiet at times. When it came time for me to go back to my family, my parents took me to the airport. It was time to say goodbye. When I looked at my dad, his blue eyes were saddened and watery; and his words were choked. This was the last time that we would see one another on this side of Heaven, and I stopped the words from coming out of my mouth. It felt better to just say a cheerful "tchau" in Portuguese, given with a big hug and an "I'm praying for you, Dad!" I wanted to avoid an emotional, drawn-out goodbye during such a difficult time filled with unknowns. Later, on the plane, I cried until I emptied my eyes of water; but I just couldn't bear my dad seeing my tears and losing all hope in the fight against cancer.

Paul and I had gifted Dad a small blue picture frame which he kept near his recliner. On it was a painting of a beautiful tree with orange-colored leaves and the words: "I cannot see the wind, but I feel its strength. I cannot see my God, but I feel His love. 'Now faith is the substance of things hoped for, the evidence of things not seen.' Hebrews 11:1."

I knew Dad's faith was in Jesus Christ—that He alone would carry him through this dark time. The months ahead would be colored with sorrow and pain; but eventually, a glorious freedom would come when Dad left this world behind.

## To Lauren E. Baughman

*You came to us*
*Like a teddy bear,*
*Gently entering our lives.*
*We were lonely and without a father,*
*Like a fish tossed in the tide.*

*We became one family—*
*Steps, halves, and wholes—*
*Gathering*
*In our many different roles.*

*You brought us to church*
*And, ultimately, God.*
*It was there we met*
*Our loving Savior*
*And the care of His staff and rod.*

# Saying Goodbye

*As adults, you let us go, one by one,*
*To find our life's paths,*
*Always there*
*When we needed you*
*And ready to welcome us back.*

*Somehow, you knew*
*When to keep quiet,*
*Even though we did things wrong.*
*You let us make our own choices.*
*And write our own songs.*

*Our children, though so many,*
*Always found a place in your lap.*
*They were welcomed and loved*
*With a smile and a laugh.*

*Your big heart not only*
*Had room for me and mine,*
*But for friends, neighbors,*
*Co-workers, sisters, aunts,*
*And many, many more,*
*Who received your loyal care*
*As a beautiful watch that keeps perfect time.*

*Thank you, Dad,*
*For all you mean to me and more.*
*We laughed and cried together.*
*I do appreciate you so.*
*Your kindnesses are too many to ignore.*

## CHAPTER 5
# Spill the Beans

*"But even the very hairs of your head are all numbered. Fear not therefore: ye are of more value than many sparrows."*

Luke 12:7

Our first year in Brazil, we were living temporarily at a vacation house in a small village called Santo Antonio de Posse. It was a very hot summer that year, and we all decided to go to a barber shop to get our hair cut. We often enjoyed finding our own way around, bumbling with limited Portuguese; and in this particular instance, we found ourselves at a tiny shop a little way off the main road.

A woman barber was there. Her hair was cut short over her ears with blondish streaks running through it, which made her large glasses seem even bigger. Paul bravely went first and then Jeremy. Being as hot as it was, the cold tap water running down over our heads felt so delicious. Then it was Isa's turn to get the ends trimmed off from her long, sandy-blonde hair. I went last. As I thought about what kind of haircut I wanted, I took some long minutes and tried to convey it in broken Portuguese to the hairdresser. I wanted only a little taken off, but not too much. I thought that I had successfully expressed how much to the hairdresser when she gave a big smile, motioned her index figure upward, and nodded, saying, "Princess Diana!"

I was not so sure what the woman had meant by that, but I was soon to find out! The hairdresser kept cutting and cutting, and I could feel most of my long hair falling softly to the floor below like feathers. At last, she was finished; and with a confident grin, she held up a mirror in the back. Looking into the mirror, I saw that my bare neck was exposed, and my hair was cut short in a style much like that of the woman barber!

It was much different than I had planned. Being restrained in the barber chair with the hairdresser and her happy scissors, there was no stopping her. It happened to be a similar haircut to Diana, the princess of Wales. I would have to get used to it. With the hot Brazilian weather, it would be cooler; and it would be so much easier. Why, I could run a small comb through it in six seconds!

"You will get used to it!" Paul said.

"It makes you look thinner!"

*Making one look thinner* happened to be something important to me, being raised in the '70s and '80s; and I accepted it as a great compliment. Though we never returned to the barber, I was satisfied with the haircut. We paid her a tip and went to buy gelato around the corner.

One beautiful day in May, soon after the trip to the barbershop, we were invited to a Brazilian barbecue by a warm-hearted, upper-class family who lived nearby. They spoke English well as a result of their studies at college, so we were able to communicate easily with them. They also had two small children, and they were fun and very caring.

We were invited on Mother's Day to enjoy the Brazilian national dish called "feijoada" for the first time. It was black bean stew with pork and rice. Black beans were usually the main star of the meals with all the other ingredients added as a condiment. When we arrived on the veranda of the large Brazilian villa, the grandmother was stirring a large cast iron pot on the fire outside; and there was a smoky smell permeating the air around the table.

The sound of Brazilian country music was playing with drawn-out vocal syllables and perfectionistic guitar chords.

We sat down at the long wooden picnic table with the rest of the family getting ready to eat. A woman server walked close by and, with a large redwood spoon, placed delicious white rice on the brown patterned plates in front of us. In the middle of the table were several bowls with an unusual combination of ingredients. There were orange slices; stewed, buttery, dark green kale; large bowls of black beans the color of muddy goo; and Brazilian farofa, which are fine breadcrumbs.

One of the sons ladled some of the black bean stew onto Paul's plate saying, "Ah ha ha! You know that we Brazilians use every single part of the pig in this soup!"

Paul looked intently into the black pot.

"Every single part?" he asked.

There was the smell of sausage and herbs with fried garlic and onions.

"Umm, yes, please!" I said tasting the dark colored mixture.

It wasn't so bad. My mother always told me that there wasn't anything that I wouldn't try. Jeremy took one look and would only eat his typical bland plate of white rice, but I also added an orange slice to help fill up his plate. Isa looked over at my plate and decided to try a few small pieces of sausage and some rice but not one bean because they were too black to taste any good, according to her. As Paul took a big bite of the famous Brazilian feijoada, he felt something slippery with his tongue; and it slid down his throat without being chewed up.

"Is it possible that there is tongue in this soup?" Paul asked.

"Oh, yes, there is!" said the son, as he elbowed the other family member sitting close by. Shaking, he could not hold in his laughter any longer.

"Bah!" Paul said with a grimace on his face. Looking at Paul caused the whole table to explode in laughter. Paul's stomach then started to churn; and feeling somewhat queasy, he reservedly pushed his plate away trying not to be noticed. He grabbed a cold drink from the bucket filled with ice and tried to wash away the unsettled feeling.

It was coming to the end of the day, and the nape of my neck began to itch with a burning sensation that I had never experienced. I tried, but I couldn't stop scratching, my long nails almost causing my skin to bleed. Time went by, but the itching sensation didn't go away. Isa looked over and started scratching her head also, and the skin behind her ears was turning pink.

Our friend, Tiana, noticed and said, "You two must have some sort of allergy. Your skin is turning reddish!"

Paul looked at my neck, then in Isa's direction, and then at his watch. "It's time to go!" he said.

We packed into our hot little car, a red Fiat, with the air conditioner on and circulating; but I continued to scratch my neck and my head all over, though it was of no use. The burning itch wouldn't go away. Paul decided to make a stop at the hospital.

A young nurse looked at my scalp first and then Isa, and she asked, "What kind of shampoo are you using?"

That was a good question. The shampoo aisle at the grocery store in Brazil was full and varied with all kinds of delicious-looking potions that were, for the most part, made from all-natural ingredients. There were all kinds of shampoos, including avocado shampoo; egg shampoo; floral shampoos; fresh, blue mint shampoo; and aloe, which was creamy and green and promised faster hair growth. I could spend an hour, at least, looking over all the different kinds. The sweet smells of the shampoos were intoxicating. One look at most of the Brazilian women, and one could spot their most beautiful feature, which was their long flowing healthy hair. The advertising on the bottles picturing women with beautiful hair led me to try the Brazilian shampoo rather than the American brand that I was used to.

I answered the nurse with a red face, "We are using an egg shampoo." I gave her the name.

"Is it yellow?" the nurse asked. Yes, indeed it was bright yellow.

"Change your shampoo, and it should take care of the problem." We went to the grocery store and bought Head and Shoulders instead. Still, the itching continued.

The next day, around ten o'clock in the morning, Isa was sent home from school with a handwritten note saying that she had head lice.

Head lice! My world went spinning out of orbit. I had never had head lice. I didn't know what it was, or how to take it off, or where it came from, for that matter. I had always thought that it was a sign of poor hygiene, and only people who were dirty would catch it. I was wrong. It was the first time that my scalp had ever seen head lice, but it wouldn't be the last. My work with little children who came from different homes would give me head lice more times than I could count. It was inevitable. With each new child came a new case of head lice.

"Take each hair and comb it very carefully with a fine iron comb," said a Brazilian woman who lived nearby.

"Let the medicine to remove the eggs rest on your hair for thirty minutes. That should take care of it!" she said. "It doesn't mean that you are dirty. Lice love to find a good clean scalp to live on. Don't worry," she reassured us.

In only a few days, I went from being "Princess Diana" to what I thought was a bum. Life would not be all glamor or adventure in Brazil. There were hard days and hard work ahead. Through it all, I grew; and I learned more deeply of the undying love of the Heavenly Father.

CHAPTER 6
# Home at Last

*"Precious in the sight of the LORD is the death of His saints."*

Psalm 116:15

From his hospital bed, Lauren's breathing was getting more and more raspy and labored as he listened to his sister, Barb, give all the lighthearted news happenings of the family. They had a special, brother-sister bond; and throughout the years, they remained close, though they never remained living in the same small town. She was the one who was with him when he passed. I was heartbroken that I couldn't be with him in his last moments, but it was a comfort to learn all these details from my aunt. My mom, his devoted wife of nineteen years would hold his tanned wrinkled hand in hers; and she would continue to pray softly. Lauren was on heavy medication for the pain, and he was in and out of consciousness. There was not a word that could make his pain go away, only her presence was available to help, as well as a prayer or two. The hospice nurse came regularly with quiet steps, checking to see if all was well.

Before my mom met Lauren, she hadn't traveled to many new places. She had never even been to the Amish town nearby with rolling hills and fresh air. They would go off for a day on their motorcycle, seeing the beautiful land of Ohio. Beyond their own state, they traveled to Hawaii, where they said that all the food and drink was served with a slice of pineapple. They took a trip to the Grand Canyon, which my mom, despite her terrible fear of heights, managed to look out over the beautiful views with a calm smile. Lauren taught Judy the joy of the journey, and now he was embarking on a very new journey of his own all alone. He would leave many loved ones behind.

As the end came near, my dad became very drowsy and tired; his eyelids began to shut under a heavy weight, blocking out the picture of my aunt before him. I imagine he thought that he would just rest his eyes for a moment. It was only for a moment—closing and resting—and the next time he opened them, he would see Heaven. His pain was completely gone.

He probably leaped up to his feet and began to run ahead with joy—something he hadn't been able to do in a very long time. In Heaven, he could skip down the lane like a child; and he could hear, clear as a bell, the singing of angelic voices. His crooked legs were straight and strong again; and unaided by his pacemaker, his heart wouldn't skip a beat. He could run down the path amid the breathtaking paradise, seeing some familiar faces who looked young and vivacious. Mary, his mother, probably greeted him with her twinkling smile.

He came to Jesus, Whose arms were stretched open wide with His nail-scarred hands, saying, "Welcome home, My son!"

> *Manchester—Lauren E. Baughman, 66, saw the gates of Heaven open wide, July 29, 2000. A lifetime resident of the Manchester area, he retired in January 1994, after thirty-eight years of service with W. G. Lockhart. With many years of heavy equipment experience, Lauren donated many hours to the Manchester community by building ball fields and churches. He was a member of Manchester Trinity Chapel, and a volunteer fireman for twenty-seven years with the Franklin Township Fire Department, and a member of the Ohio Operating Engineers Local 18 since 1956.*[3]

---

3  "Obituaries," *Akron Beacon Journal*, July 30, 2000.

## CHAPTER 7
# Lost in the Dark

*"And the light shineth in darkness; and the darkness comprehended it not."*

John 1:5

## Jaguariúna, Brazil
### 2000

Time passed by very quickly in Brazil. Old things were passing away, and new things were beginning. New revelations opened in the eyes of my heart to the world around me, as well as to the person that I was at the time. I realized that I had a passion deep inside to help the poor and that in my years of sadness, God was always there. I began to love Brazil and continued to feel at home in this beautiful, mysterious land. I loved the many-colored people and the varied culture.

Brazil is a land of many influences—European, African, and even native Indian. I was drawn to the spectacular nature around me like the coffee growing on the trees of the farm nearby or the bird of paradise—a flowering plant that seemed too pretty to be real and almost looked like plastic in its creation. I never grew tired of the umbrella trees with their bright, orange-red colored flowers. There was always something blooming; and it was always green, no matter what season of the year it was. God was always faithful. We came by faith, looking for a new place to live; and God was helping us find our way, slowly.

Sometimes, the loneliness seemed to engulf me. I couldn't speak the native language of Portuguese, though I tried and tried. I didn't have anyone to talk to—only Jesus. I spent my days listening intently to distinguish a Portuguese word to be able to enter the fast, steady flow of the conversation with the Brazilian people around me, but most of the time, I was completely lost. Our little family of four was often a small English-speaking bubble in the vast terrain of Portuguese. It was very lonely for me. At times, I doubted myself, thinking that I didn't have what it took to be a missionary.

I asked the Lord many times to help me with the language. We did have the occasional friend drop by from the city who had learned English. I waited for those meetings and soaked up the fellowship like a sponge. It was hard to trust God for the grace of each new day. I felt completely isolated and out of place where we were living in a small shack on a farm in rural Brazil.

When we first entered the primitive shack where we would live, the first thing that I noticed was the terrible smell, like the musty smell of an old chest of drawers. Whatever I did, I couldn't get rid of the smell of that little house. The cold cement floors were painted bright yellow, and whenever the children or myself walked barefoot on them, the soles of our feet would be stained with the color. The kitchen was small and the bathroom barely usable, and the window openings didn't have any glass. We learned that a home without any glass was easy for all kinds of critters to enter. On a cold rainy night, Jeremy found a red coral snake, the most poisonous snake in our region of Brazil. He didn't touch it, he only cried out, "Snake, snake!" Paul quickly ran in with a broom to exterminate it. Next, we found a scorpion hiding in a coffee mug, and poisonous spiders were high up in the rafters, spinning lots of webs.

We were given a second-hand fridge that looked like it had been made in the fifties. It was cute until one night Paul was given a strong shock when he reached for the handle in the dark to get something to drink. We quickly traded it in for a new one.

We were given a Siamese cat, and it disappeared into the woods. We looked and searched, but we couldn't find it; and later on, two more cats of ours disappeared.

In spite of everything, Paul flourished with the language. He learned Portuguese from the children he worked with without ever opening a textbook. I tried studying and only seemed to get more behind in learning until someone told me, in Brazil, there are many types of Portuguese; and there were many ways to say a phrase. While I had been painstakingly studying, I was learning the very formal way to speak Portuguese, which we never heard at work or during our day-to-day lives. In studying and working so hard on my Portuguese, I fell behind.

The deafening silence around me, as well as the loudness of a language that I couldn't understand, led me to my journal; and I filled a page every day. The only person that I could talk to, other than my small family, was Jesus. The days and months flew by so fast, and because of the business of caring for our family, I often was forgetful of the date. The boys who were left in our care at the farm captured my heart, which kept me going in the most difficult of circumstances, and I could see with my own eyes how God was working in their lives after we brought them in.

Once the rainy season was over, the Baptist church was able to finish construction on a new house where we were to live. It was a beautiful little house with nice windows and floors. I loved the kitchen that was built, and the large veranda in the front was the perfect place for the children to play. Best of all, it had good insulation that protected us from any critters.

I slowly swept the dust off the veranda, and then I watered the garden with a thick green hose. I then put on some music and began to dance alone. At the isolated little house, there was no one nearby who would be watching.

After the death of my dad, Lauren, my emotions were up and down; and some days, I felt so isolated. I put on my earthly armor, hiding my heart deep beneath those around me. Worship held a key for victory; and when I had some time alone, I would play worship music, many times in English with the songs that I had learned back home.

"Saudade" is a word used in Brazil, which completely described what I was going through. "Saudade" is defined as a feeling of longing, melancholy, or nostalgia.[4] I grieved for my dad, and I missed not being there with my family when he passed away. I also missed the community in Amsterdam, where we had lived and made strong friendships like the bonds of brotherhood that would endure through time. It was like untangling the cords of many emotions; but slowly, everything began to get better. It was hard to see my way through; but gradually, things started to become clearer.

Though I began to love this new land of Brazil, I was not feeling at home yet. I was traveling through—an outsider, a "gringo"—and at times, I was the center of unwanted attention and the naïve victim of a cunning thief. My little family was often watched and put on display as if we were living in a glass house. We needed our privacy, and we needed the peace of being at home.

The feeling of not belonging nagged my emotions at regular intervals. Although I was an American living in the Netherlands, I did have a European heritage—my dad was Romanian—and I found safety and comfort with my European friends. In Brazil, being a missionary, I seemed to be put on a pedestal that was not of my liking; and it was something that I was not accustomed to. When I went into town, every pair of eyes seemed to be on me, whether I was good or bad, pretty or ugly. I was vulnerable and had personal struggles that I kept deep inside. Like a daisy that had been roughly transplanted to hot, rocky soil only to wilt and bend low to the ground, I was feeling low and exhausted.

---

4   Oxford English Dictionary, s.v. "saudade (n.)," July 2023, https://doi.org/10.1093/OED/7334082726.

I learned during this dark night of the soul that I had a strong enemy, Satan, who would tempt me in every way possible to get me to quit and go home. He was slippery, deceitful, cunning, and cruel. Deep inside, I wanted to pack up and go back home to Ohio. I was ready to give up on myself and on our calling. The angels in Heaven must have shuddered a little when they saw how close I came to running away from it all and throwing away, with my own hand, the promises that God had made. I nearly missed all the wonderful blessings that He had in store for Paul and me and our children.

> *"Surely, He shall deliver thee from the snare of the fowler, And from the noisome pestilence. He shall cover thee with His feathers, and under His wings shalt thou trust: His truth shall be thy shield and buckler."*
>
> Psalm 91:3-4

During this dark night of the soul, when I could not see that bright and shining future that was just ahead, I learned to persevere and not give up; and though we couldn't see clearly with our vision blurred by the difficulties all around us, God was with us. Sometimes, when I felt like I couldn't go one step further, the Lord carried me and kept me from falling.

> *"Now unto Him that is able to keep you from falling, and to present you faultless before the presence of His glory with exceeding joy, to the only wise God our Savior, be glory and majesty, dominion and power, both now and ever. Amen."*
>
> Jude 1:24-25

It was at this time in my life that I began battling many spiritual pressures. I had many fears for my future. It was the year that we had rain every day for many weeks. It was a nice soothing rain, but it also caused the road to Holambra to be impassable. We had to find another way to go into town to take the children to school. The rain left us isolated, and the monotony of it occurring everyday created a weight of sadness on my shoulders. I longed to see the sun come out once again.

In Brazil, I was learning that not everything was as it seemed; people were not always what they projected themselves to be. A part of the culture was meticulously caring about the outward appearance, which distracted an outsider—at least, at first—from that person's true character. There were predators around who were skilled at using a beautiful mask. There were cobras, who, at the first chance, would bite and fill you with poison; and scorpions, who acted like they were dead only to sting your hand when you reached out, leaving you with a long-lasting pain. We needed the wisdom of God to discern who was who.

Paul started to get stressed and had not been himself. He always had the project with the street boys on his mind. He worked until it was dark, and Isa and Jeremy were ready to go to bed. He walked over the hill to our little house, exhausted of energy and barely able to give our own two children the attention they needed. We didn't have any time to really talk; but instead, we only bickered back and forth like a couple of chickens. Strangely, there were times when we couldn't agree on anything. The stress continued to build like a castle of sand.

I came to the school to pick up Jeremy, and he started to cry.

"What is it, son?" I was embarrassed that he didn't want to go home yet.

He continued to cry and shook his head.

Finally, through persistence, I managed to get him into the car. *Why didn't my son want to come home?* The frustration ate at my thoughts until later in the day Isa, Jeremy, and I erupted in anger—all three of us frustrated and upset over something small. Paul was unable to get away from work on the project, and I wasn't managing very well on my own.

I turned on the worship music and filled up their swimming pool to help us enjoy the afternoon better. I went to the Lord and prayed; and peace came, washing away all the anger and tortured frustration. As I looked to the flowers, I remembered about God's care of them. I had to trust Him; He would not let me down.

During that time of feeling utterly lost, the Lord began giving me more of an understanding of how I fit into the big plan. I also began to see Paul more through the Lord's eyes, and I understood why he did the things he did. Paul and I often saw things differently. Our personalities were opposites in many ways; and because of a lack of understanding toward each other, our marriage was tense during that time.

"Paul, I want to go home to Ohio!" I heard myself say after another difficult day alone. I truly felt that I could not make it any longer.

Paul's downcast expression made me take back my words and give it just a little more time. All I could do was to stand and trust God for His deliverance. I waited for a miracle.

> "Wherefore take unto you the whole armor of God, that ye may be able to withstand in the evil day, and having done all, to stand. Stand therefore."
>
> Ephesians 6:13-14

A few weeks later at a service by the Baptist church that we worked with, Paul took out a little square of note paper and wrote me an apology.

"I'm sorry, Jill," he wrote. "I promise to do better in the future."

It was everything that I needed to hear to keep believing in him and his work with children. When a Dutch man makes a promise, you know that he means it. The Dutch are not ones who speak empty words, but they are direct and guided by truth.

I spent the best part of my days with our own children, Isa and Jeremy, speaking mainly English. Even though we lived in a little shack at the time, our children were well-dressed, carried brand-new school bags, and had well-groomed hair when they went to school. They wore clean, crisp uniforms with white tennis shoes. It was a chance for them to get into town and away from the farm. Isa and Jeremy made friends and seemed to enjoy the day away from the muddy, rustic grounds of the isolated, rural place where we had been living. Paul, being more extraverted and outgoing, learned the language rapidly; and we were able to navigate around town and with the Brazilian people.

We grew in the realization of the importance of not being isolated from the other families and the community. We became friends with people of the Dutch community in Holambra, as well as the Brazilians, whom we grew to love. Rather than running away from the challenges, we needed to learn to face those challenges, attacking the walls brick by brick and removing stone upon stone. One day, we would arrive at cultural integration. One day, we would be more at home in this new spacious place called Brazil.

During our time in the neighborhood of Guedes, we became accustomed to the churches in Brazil. Many times, there was a dress code that we learned to follow. My Portuguese was not developed far enough for me to understand any of the sermons or to talk with the brothers and sisters, but I loved the simple songs that they would sing. The Brazilians would sing with passion, though out of tune; and I remember in particular a song about diving into the Holy Spirit and how powerful it was. The melancholic tone was beautiful and healing in its sound. Even though I could only speak a greeting in Portuguese, the Brazilian brothers and sisters always greeted us with warm hugs and even kisses. I couldn't understand the long prayers that they prayed over me, but I felt their power.

During the night, there were strange sounds coming from the neighbor's nearby woods which caused me to remember some talk that there were people who practiced witchcraft in our part of rural Brazil. The spiritual pressure was heavy, and I began to know terror more than I had before.

"Macumba exists in Brazil. There are those who do witchcraft and cast spells on the Christians doing the work of the Lord," Pastor Roberto had told us. He was the lead pastor of a large Baptist church, who had asked us to come and work with them in Brazil.

*Macumba* is a term used to describe various religions of the African diaspora found in Brazil, Argentina, Uruguay, and Paraguay. It is sometimes considered by non-practitioners to be a form of witchcraft or black magic. The events that took place those first years in Brazil caused enormous amount of stress that I was unable to process until much later. Some days, it seemed as if Hell had been pushing against us. We were having one bad day after another. I didn't know whom I could trust. The trauma of these difficulties left a scar, a stutter, and an insecurity—or fear—of man.

One of these difficulties came when we welcomed in a stranger who presented himself as a friend; but in reality, this "friend" was like a jaguar—deadly and alert. He seemed friendly enough; but as time went on, it became clear that the kindness was attached to another motive. Though the jaguar gave the outward appearance of a religious leader and a pillar of the community, there was just something that didn't feel right—like a bell rung slightly out of tune.

I went to the Lord and prayed, and there were alarm bells loudly ringing. We had a limited number of people we could talk to, which drew us even closer into intimacy with this jaguar, whose only wish was to see us fail, pack up, and go back to the Netherlands. I had accidentally walked into his territory; and upon coming closer, I felt afraid all the way to my core. There was no way to fight him, and the best that I could do was to slowly come back out of his territory and stay only in mine.

The jaguar must not be underestimated in the least as to the amount of havoc that he could create in our lives. Destruction seemed to follow his path. The jaguar worked very hard at presenting himself as a helpful friend, trading little personal tidbits in order to pursue knowledge about us. We readily gave out information like a child who hands over his painting, not knowing how it would be received by the rest of the world. Like a cobra, the jaguar was efficient in planting a little poison with its bite, causing me to doubt God, people, and myself. I had no hard evidence—only feelings—but those feelings set off a million alarms dressed in red flags. I felt the danger all around me. I could only stay quiet and trust the Lord. There was no one who could help.

After it was over and we went our separate ways from the jaguar, I struggled for a long time when I spoke the Portuguese language with people I didn't know. I was afraid of saying the wrong thing to the wrong person. I stumbled over the fear of how people would perceive me. Years later, when I began to study God's Word about His grace and love, I finally found my voice again. I was healed from my fear of speaking and the stumbling over words when I tried to express myself to others. God delivered me from my fear of man. I was finally free.

I was even able to forgive the jaguar and to understand better what had taken place as the Lord even healed my memories. To this day, I don't know how we survived everything that transpired at the farm in Guedes; but I know that the Lord protected us.

Living in Brazil, I saw injustice throughout the land as many complained of corruption. I learned like the other Christians not to seek revenge or justice whenever I was wronged.

"Put it in God's hands," they would say. "Justice belongs to the Lord." I lived by that, and I didn't seek revenge for what happened. I forgave and extended mercy and grace instead of retribution. I didn't seek justice—that was up to God. Everything that this jaguar did to us came crashing back to meet him. I could walk away in peace, able to enjoy all the blessings that the Lord had for me living in Brazil.

## CHAPTER 8
## A New Day

*"For, lo, the winter is past, the rain is over and gone; The flowers appear on the earth; the time of the singing of birds is come."*

Song of Songs 2:11-12

When the night for me couldn't get much darker, a new dawn awakened; and soon, the darkness fled. God had answered all our prayers. He guided us to a new, broader path. It was a new day! The past year would only remain a painful memory. That trial was over now. We were about to move to a new place, where God would richly supply all our needs.[5] He was sending us help, and we would not remain alone; we would grow. At the time, I struggled with fears and had a hunger for community; but God guided us to this new place where He would plant us, and He protected us and parted the waves so that we could walk right through.

I held the rectangular sky-blue tin in my hands. It had a painting of colorful flowers on the front of it, and it looked vintage. It was a pencil box given to me for my thirty-sixth birthday by Rodrigo, the first little boy who came to live at the children's shelter during a troubled time in his childhood.

"Happy birthday!" he said with a shy smile that shined from his tanned face.

---
5   Philippians 4:19

I gave him a hug, and I thanked him for such a unique gift. It was something that had probably been given to him that he, in turn, gave away.

On the tin pencil box, it read, *The springtime of life, Make the best of your time.* It was a practical gift, and I loved it and kept it with me always. It reminded me of that very first boy who came to live at our children's home.

The following month, Rodrigo was happily reunited with his father; and he grew up to be a good man with a lovely wife. He once came for a visit to Lar Feliz after quite some years; and he asked Paul and me, "Do you remember me?"

"Of course!" We remembered his open smile and the kindness that flowed out of his good heart. How could we forget the first boy of many who would come to the children's home, which would later be named Lar Feliz or, in English, "Happy Home?"

Lar Feliz was first born on the papers of my journal. As I read through the Scriptures about small beginnings, and how the Lord would give the increase,[6] I felt the Lord nudging me that this would happen for our project, and it did. The Lord quickly made a way for us to move to a more organized place close by Holambra and Isa and Jeremy's school. It was a miracle to me—like the parting of the Red Sea—the Lord led us to a better place, and He provided everything that we would need. The farm that we moved to even had the exact number of beds for the children. This was where we would begin to build.

Lar Feliz was officially born on the second of May, and God continued to bless and to prosper our goals through extraordinary gifts from unexpected visitors. We became landowners when we received a visit from a doctor and his wife from Cleveland, Ohio. We had been looking at a property that was for rent and located catty-cornered from the farm that we had been currently renting. When we checked the price of the rent, it was too high; but the doctor and his wife paid for the land with cash. Paul saw the need to have more rooms to broaden our doors to not only little boys but also girls and infants. God provided everything at the right hour. Not long afterward,

---

[6]  1 Corinthians 3:6-7

a Dutch couple came to visit; and they bought us the first farm that we had been renting. Owning two functioning farms was only the beginning of the prosperity that God blessed Lar Feliz with. He is a good Father Who loves His children.

Though we originally came to work beside a Baptist church from Campinas, God gave us the faith to become independent and to form our own non-profit organization in Brazil. It was a lot of paperwork, and every detail was thought through. We were discouraged by the Baptist church, at first, to become independent; but later, they gave us their blessing. Even though we would no longer work together, we parted as friends. Our vision was different than theirs, though we had learned a lot from them. We would eventually grow much more, and the Lord would draw the best of the Brazilians as staff to partner with us and transform Lar Feliz into a prosperous institution that helped many children and changed lives. It would last for decades.

The following is from the Lar Feliz handbook:

> *Lar Feliz, a sheltering home, was founded with the arrival of Paul van Opstal and his wife, Jill, to Brazil. Through the years, Lar Feliz experienced many changes. Initially, they received only boys. Today, Lar Feliz is a shelter for all children and adolescents who have been taken away from high-risk situations where they are vulnerable.*

> *The mission of Lar Feliz is to equip children and adolescents with the skills needed to become capable adults, exercising their citizenship; establishing relationships; and permitting them to have the best conditions of life. When possible, the children are returned to their biological family or extended family; but sometimes adoption into a new family is necessary.*

> *The children and adolescents that live at Lar Feliz range in age from zero to eighteen; and they come from families that lack protection and care, permitting them to be exposed to situations of risk and maltreatment. The length of stay at Lar Feliz for these children and*

*adolescents depends on a dynamic change in the family situation and is evaluated by the shelter and judicial powers.*[7]

Moving from Guedes to a farm on the edge of Holambra was a change from night to day. The uncertainty was over, and we began to build. Our family pulled up the tent stakes of life, moved to a small town where everyone knew their neighbor, and traded isolation for a community. We were welcomed into Dutch-Brazilian cultural groups, and the blessings started coming. We began raising support from the USA and the Netherlands; but soon, awareness was raised in our town. Many churches, organizations, and schools provided support in numerous ways. Being isolated at the first farm in Guedes taught us many things—the most important was to come to the end of ourselves and rely fully on God. The light at the end of the long, dark night was grasping His hand in trust and allowing Him to lead on.

---

[7] Solange Wagner and Paul van Opstal, *Lar Feliz Handbook* (Cosmopolis: The Happy Home Project, 2001).

CHAPTER 9
# Forming a Dream Team

*Home is where love resides,*
*Memories are created,*
*Friends always belong,*
*Laughter never ends.*

(author unknown)

When we moved to our new location, we made an organized plan. Solange Wagner and my husband, Paul, were able to write out projects that would benefit the children and raise funds and awareness of our work. Solange, our psychologist, was a valuable member of the team who brought order and excellence to our work with children. She also drew in other psychologists and social workers who did extraordinary work, forming our dream team at Lar Feliz.

The functioning of the home depended very much on teamwork. Lar Feliz is cared for by a technical team, who work as a liaison between the children, the judicial system, and the natural parents. This group, consisting of psychologists and social workers, ensures the children's rights.

Cristiane Cravo, a social worker at Lar Feliz, described to me how a typical visit to a troubled home would be. Whenever she entered a home, she had to check for specific things like the child's basic rights, their health, and their education. One sign that things were not going well in the home was that physical violence or sexual abuse occurred and a family member didn't recognize it. This showed a lack of responsibility. Cris has a sharp intuition, and she has made many visits to troubled homes for her work at Lar Feliz. I have always known her heart of defending the children's rights. It is what makes her work so effective.

The children who entered the baby house perhaps came on the worst day of their young lives. It was noted that toddlers and babies in Brazil were not taken out of their homes for little or no reason. Often, it was a very dark, grave reason, where small children had suffered unimaginable abuse and neglect already in their living situations; and for most of the children who came to Lar Feliz, alcohol or drug addiction was a factor.

In a typical institution for children, one negative aspect is that the ratio of children to caregivers is high, resulting in aggression. A sign of this problem can be aggression in the child, hostility, and a lack of bonding.

As a result, we hired many new workers who would be able to give each individual child all the love needed to heal. We ensured that there would be lots of activities where the children could learn; and in learning, they would explore the talents that they had within them. Every birthday was celebrated, and each child had their own set of clothes.

Daiane Lopez was a new social worker on staff at Lar Feliz. She is tiny but statured with greatness in her mind and character. Recently graduated from a rigorous, five-year program, she would learn how to put the freshly learned theories into practice.

One afternoon, I asked Daiane how she went about her work. She shared with me that during her first week at Lar Feliz, a child arrived—a nine-year-old boy. She remembered the golden rule of the importance of listening to a child when he arrives. Important information can be gained just by listening.

"How do you like school?" she asked.

"I never go."

"Here at Lar Feliz, Pastor Paul makes sure that everyone goes to school. You will enjoy it!"

Daiane began the paper chase of gathering his identification and birth certificate that she would need to enroll the new boy in school. She called to have a medical card made for when he would go to the doctor for regular checkups.

She walked over to the home where the boys stayed that was later named *The House of Friendship*. She would like to try to find out from the monitor there if the boy showed any interest in a particular subject.

"Does he know how to swim?" she asked as her eyes traveled to the nearby pool where the children learned to swim.

"Not yet, but I'm sure that he will learn like all the children do when they come. He's not afraid of the water, not a bit!"

"We have art lessons on Monday, and we have music lessons on Tuesday. Let's see how he likes to participate in those!"

Each member of the technical team, which included Daiane, had a large amount of office work. A PIA, or "plan of action," needed to be scrambled out on the computer. The boy's mother would visit on Friday at Lar Feliz. Daiane and the psychologist, Rodrigo, would interview the mother to check if she was able to find work. Any sign of chemical addiction would be considered. Statistically, over 90 percent of the children who came to Lar Feliz had one or both parents who were addicted to drugs or alcohol. A family that was poor in Brazil could still be happy; but when either the mother or father decided to use drugs, it became unlivable for the children involved.

A net was created in the earlier years of Lar Feliz that helped us to see where the parents had gone for help in the past. A sense of teamwork was profitable for everyone to know what was going on and how best to help the family. It was important to know what had already been tried to be more effective in productive therapy.

"Addicted to cocaine," was written on the record of the little boy's father, who had been in rehab over the past months. The mother was without any hope of support from her family; and they were left starving in a place of squalor without hope for tomorrow. A teacher who had missed the boy at school filed a report to the children's protection agency, and a home inspection was made.

After the inspection, the information was gathered, signed by the agent who made the inspection, and sent to the judge of the children's court to determine whether the child could stay at home. The judge decided to remove the boy from the home after it was determined that the family was living in a high risk of danger or death. Living in filth without food or water and missing school were all signs that he was not in the best care at home. He was brought to Lar Feliz.

In a month's time, there would be an afternoon meeting, where the judge and the officials would ask lots of questions about the progress of the boy. The plan in action always included working with the natural parents, helping them better their situation to return the boy back home. There were times when this day would happen, but there were also times when the child would have to be placed for adoption after giving the parents chance after chance.

"I want to go home," said almost every child who came to Lar Feliz. Children had cloudy memories of the bad times they had endured. These children often had the gift of trust and forgiveness toward the adults in their lives, whether this was deserved or not. Most of the time, a child always defended his mother, no matter what.

This was the typical day of a social worker in Lar Feliz. With wisdom, a wonderful home is built; and at Lar Feliz, we were entrusted with children whose homes were broken by foolishness. Every single person had an important part to play in the grand scheme of caring for a multitude of children who would come and go. Some would stay for a longer period, and others with extended family members would stay for shorter amounts of time.

## CHAPTER 10
# Life Inside of the Home

*"Train up a child in the way he should go: and when he is old, he will not depart from it."*

Proverbs 22:6

She was a sweet-faced eight-year-old girl named Anna with light brown hair and light, creamy-looking skin.

"Where's my mother?" asked Anna.

Her brown eyes filled with tears. "Where is she?" she asked with more insistence.

The staff at the baby house didn't have an answer. We were forbidden to allow the children of the home to call us "mother"—that much was clear. The rules had been stipulated that we were not even allowed to tell a new child to "feel at home" when they arrived at Lar Feliz. It was encouraged not to make strong connections with any child.

We understood the reasoning behind this because the children never stayed permanently. They were just passing through. Sometimes, they were leaving high risk situations; and then they would go back to a better home and healed family. Other times, they would be placed for adoption and receive a new family. Lar Feliz was just an in-between place, like a hospital, where they would heal.

We understood what we couldn't say, but what could we say? How could we comfort this crying child who, for days, kept asking for her mother? We took her on outings at an animal farm, and we found ways to distract her. Because of the seriousness of the situation of Anna's home, it was highly unlikely that she would go back there. Rather, she and her older brother would be placed for adoption.

We tried everything that we could think of; but still, the little girl would cry and ask for her mother. I had a thought as I remembered my aunts who were lovely and caring. In Brazil, it was customary to call teachers and adults working with children by the names "tía" or "tío"—the equivalent to "aunt" or "uncle" in English.

I looked into the eyes of the sobbing little girl, and simply said, "Here at Lar Feliz, we only have aunts—not mothers—but aunts are very special people. They look out for you, and they love you when no one else is around."

The little girl's crying finally stopped, and she gave a little laugh and a hug and began to play outside.

It was a crisp morning across the rolling hills of farm country in Jaguariúna. Tía Milene had the toddlers washed and clothed in their play clothes. They sat on the weakened, gray couch watching cartoons while nudging one another now and then.

"Wait a minute!" Milene exclaimed, bringing order once again to the living room located adjacent to the kitchen. The children were about to go on a picnic, and they could hardly contain themselves. She carefully placed a heavy oblong pan of lasagna into the oven. The delicious smell of ground beef, tomato sauce, peas, corn, ham, and mozzarella cheese permeated the room. She carefully stirred a large, shiny metal pot on the stove filled with rice. The seasonings of garlic and onions brought tears to her eyes.

The children looked forward to picnic day with all their might—so much so, they could barely sleep the night before. Diaper bags were packed with extra clothes, and a nutritious lunch was brought by car with juice and cookies for an afternoon snack. I loaded all the food and clothes—and an infant or two—into my little car and drove over to the first farm where Lar Feliz had originated. There, abundant mango trees shaded the soft grass beneath our feet. The guesthouse was nice and neat with a paved sidewalk and swimming pool in the back. It had a large kitchen, where we could heat up our food and keep the drinks cold in the fridge. The older children would walk down from the baby house on the sunny country road, passing by hibiscus flowers and a horse ranch on their way. Selma, one of the childcare workers, came walking on foot with the children, bringing her small pocketknife just in case they came across a few ripened mangos on the way.

Thankfully, a few large, lopsided ones had just fallen on the ground. The children picked them up; and Selma carefully carved the peeling off the sweet, sticky, fragrant fruit. The children came around in a circle, each one waiting for a little bit of the soft deliciousness. They ate three or four mangos in a few minutes, leaving behind traces of bright orange coloring on their lips.

The children and the workers formed a line and walked the rest of the short distance to the farm. The morning light and breeze meant that it was just right for walking, not too hot and not too cold. They sang a song on the way. Intermingled with the Brazilian staff were two Dutch volunteers, Sanne and Roosje, who were glad to take the hand of a small child or carry him on the hip the rest of the walk when he grew too tired. Once the grand gate of the farm was opened, a few of the little boys started to run, thinking about the cool waters of the swimming pool where they were headed.

Before swimming, they would have a look at the animals on the farm. There were many chickens walking around loose in the pen, and there were a few furry bunnies held in cages. The children would carefully pet and pick up the animals, which sometimes led to squeals of delight. There was an old horse that would pull a buggy, and each child got a ride. The walks in nature along the wooded path would calm the nerves of the children and the workers alike. Their laughter came a little more freely as they splattered in the pool. Their appetites were hearty with the warm food given after concentrated play. It was the best of days had by children and adults alike, the kind of time that makes golden memories that never fade.

They would swim together, eat lasagna, and swim again—though the little ones would take naps—until the time came for them to head back home. The following evening, the whole house would enjoy a deep sleep without making as much as a peep. At the end of the picnic day outing, the children who had come from situations of suffering laughed just a little bit easier, talked a little bit more, and slept peacefully without crying in the night.

It was her birthday. The little girl had an angel face and a short afro pinned in place with pink ribbons at the sides. She had been left on a lonely road to fend for herself while her mother was away. She was sexually assaulted more than once before she was picked up from her home one day by a social worker after a teacher had notified the childcare protection system—an organization that provided a net of help to catch those who had fallen. She found herself at Lar Feliz.

It was strange for her at first, and she sat on my lap for an hour until she finally got to know the other "tías." At Lar Feliz, she grew in confidence and beauty; and her favorite pastime was painting pictures. She laughed and joked around with the other children and the workers.

Today of all days was the decision for her case. It was her birthday; and it was also the day of the children's court hearings, where her case would be heard before the judge. She had on a fresh summer dress. She rode with me in my little car the short distance to the first farm where the case was held and organized by the staff at Lar Feliz. We walked past a neat row of orchids, and the smell of coffee was in the air as we made our way to the sitting room. Once we arrived at the audience, she sat only for a moment to say hello to the judge; then she was whisked away to go back to the baby house. On the way back, I unavoidably saw the broken face of the little girl's mother sobbing in the open and kneeling to the ground, while her child's eyes were averted in the back seat of the car.

Back at Lar Feliz, there was a surprise party awaiting the little girl, with balloons of all colors hanging from the ceiling and one of Tía Milene's delicious chocolate coconut cakes. She was crying softly to herself, sensing that something was not quite right. The tears of the mother meant, in fact, that she would not be going home ever again. She brushed them away as she blew out the candles after the whole baby house sang, "Congratulations to you, congratulations to you, congratulations to you dear Rachel, congratulations to you!"

She drank what was left of cold soda from a paper cup and quickly unwrapped her present, which was a baby doll made from shiny plastic with a pink mouth, a thin flowered dress, yellow hair, and big, round eyes. All the rest of the toddlers were exclaiming with delight and wanting just to touch the new doll.

The little girl left Lar Feliz a few months later to live with an attractive aunt, who had a house some distance away. Rachel took with her some new clothes, a picture book filled with photos, some colored pencils and coloring books in a hand-sewn bag, and three pairs of shoes. She received a letter from the baby house filled with messages of love that the "tías" had written to wish her success, and there were prayers of blessings over her new life. She also carried with her a homemade quilt with blue and red colors that was made with prayer by a sewing circle of women from Ohio. She was leaving us but finally found a home.

CHAPTER 11

# The Blessing of Abraham

*"By faith Abraham, when he was called to go out into a place which he should after receive for an inheritance, obeyed; and he went out, not knowing whither he went."*

Hebrews 11:8

## Holambra

June 9, 2007

The doorbell rang, and I rushed out to see who it was. A tall, blondish man wearing a business suit and a wide grin waited on the street. His name was Pastor John van Harn, and he would soon become a new friend. He was American from Dutch heritage, and he taught on the wisdom of God—the principal thing. He would share in several Brazilian churches during his stay. He always kept a full schedule during his time in Holambra. As we walked along the lands of the farms at Lar Feliz with Pastor John, we swapped stories back and forth. Paul told him about how we had arrived in Brazil with only eight suitcases in our keep.

"No!" Pastor John said. "That's not true at all!"

"What do you mean?" Paul asked. "Of course, it's true!"

"No!" said the pastor. "You came with eight suitcases and the blessing of God!"

"Yeah, you're right!" Paul said with a gleam on his face.

Many times, after that day when Paul shared about how we came to Brazil, he remembered what Pastor John said; and he shared, "We came to Brazil with eight suitcases and the blessing of the Lord!"

A dilapidated, old Ford pulled into the driveway at Lar Feliz, where Paul was waiting to receive a family of three boys. It was easy to recognize the signs of despair that so often came with the new arrivals. They plopped out of the social worker's car, their bare feet unprotected from the hot sidewalk. They had not bathed in a while; and as they scratched their heads, one could only imagine that they were filled with head lice. The brothers had only one set of clothes to their names. The social service car drove away, and the boys hung their heads as if wondering what would happen next.

Paul knelt on his knees beside them and said, "You don't have any shoes?"

The oldest of the three brothers slowly shook his head as his watery eyes stared at the ground.

"Well, we can pray about that!" he told them, and they joined hands and bowed their heads.

"Father, we thank you so much for loving us! You know what we need, Heavenly Father, even before we ask for it. Will You provide clothing and shoes for these three brothers and the extra milk that we need for the project? We thank you in advance for your provision, Lord. Amen!"

They opened their eyes and then headed to get something to eat for breakfast. Suddenly, an unknown car pulled into the drive. A large, ruddy man jumped out and pulled out two cardboard boxes and a large bag out of his car.

"Here's a donation for you!" he said with a wave. And leaving the boxes on the sidewalk, he got into his car and drove away.

Paul and a monitor walked over and picked up the boxes to find that they were filled with children's clothes and shoes. He picked up the shoes and brought them over to the boys.

"Here are some shoes for you. Why don't you try them on?"

There were three pairs of nearly new shoes the exact size of what each boy needed. They eagerly put them on and began to smile, melting away their anxiety. Later in the day, an older Dutch farmer came by with a black and white cow that would provide fresh milk for all the children. It was one of the special ways that God worked on their behalf.

Many prayers were prayed over Lar Feliz: prayers of provision, prayers for the children who came, and prayers for their families when they would go. Lar Feliz, a non-profit organization, had only 70 percent of their financial needs paid for by the government of the different towns. The rest of the money and materials needed had to be raised. It came from everywhere, and it came from unexpected sources. It came from churches, and it came from clubs. The donations often came from Brazil; but sometimes, they came from other countries. Regardless, they came. The Lord provided everything that was needed.

One morning, Paul had been in the garden, meditating on 1 Corinthians 2:9: *"But as it is written, eye hath not seen, nor ear heard, neither have entered into the heart of man, the things which God hath prepared for them that love him."*

When Paul and I arrived that morning at Lar Feliz, Sonia, the secretary, had some terrible news. She told us that the city, whose twenty-two children we cared for, owed us 135,000 reais and had decided not to pay. They said that they were short of funds, and they just didn't have it.

It took a lot to shake up my husband, but at this news, Paul grabbed the chair nearby and quickly sat down in it. If we couldn't raise that money, Lar Feliz might be forced to close. Each city signed a contract promising payment for the work of caring for the children placed in the home, but sometimes those contracts were tossed aside by the political officials. This money paid for the salaries of the workers, the food, and the clothing. One thing that it didn't pay for was a salary for Paul. He had been a volunteer, working without a salary and living from donations his whole career.

After Paul got the news that the city would not be paying, he quickly typed out that verse from 1 Corinthians 2:9, copied it on a large white paper, and taped it to the window of the main office. Everyone did what they could do, and that was to pray.

Within a week, all the money that was needed came in; and all the bills were paid. It was the Lord Who came through by preparing a financial miracle. Lar Feliz was the work of the Lord; and no matter what was going on in the economy, everything was always provided for down to the last detail. Lar Feliz was blessed in order to be a blessing. The ability to show generosity toward other ministries with what was left over—including donations of food to three different rehab homes nearby—was truly the hand of God.

## CHAPTER 12
## Stitched Up

*"But grow in grace, and in the knowledge of our Lord and Saviour Jesus Christ. To him be the glory both now and forever. Amen."*

2 Peter 3:18

Our little family that was transplanted from Holland to Holambra continued to grow in grace and favor with God. During the first years of living in Brazil, our family moved from house to house. Nothing quite fit for us until one day, we thought we had found our dream home that was available for rent with an option to buy. It was located on a main road called Tulip Avenue, and it was constructed in the early years of Holambra with tall ceilings and a large front porch. It was shaded with tall palms that swayed back and forth. There was an ample backyard where Jeremy and Isa could play catch, have friends over, and sit in the shade. We moved in, redoing the driveway and planting gardens at the side and front of the house, making everything exactly how we would want it to be for our permanent home. We were so excited!

Lar Feliz was growing into a large, fully established institution that at one time housed ninety-nine children in total. At that point, it was no longer possible for us to live as we had on the farm together with the project because we had no private family space. The home located on the first farm received building teams from the US, Canada, and the Netherlands. We began helping children from around twenty different towns in the region. We grew in donations and expertise, and we had a very professional staff that cared for the caregivers of Lar Feliz. Each person began to see the importance of gaining constant training in methods to best educate the children who had gone through traumas.

We saw the results. Lives were changed; and at times, whenever possible, whole families were healed and restored. When the immediate families of the children resisted the necessary changes required to make it possible for the children to return to their homes, the children were sent for adoption to families who were ready to love. It was there where they received the best opportunity to have a happy, successful life. They were given happy homes, but the van Opstal family was still in the process of finding our own permanent home.

Dick and his wife, Jill, from Ohio loved the work that Paul and I were doing at Lar Feliz. Being a retired principal at a public school, he loved any work that was helping, nourishing, and educating children. He organized several construction teams that came in the early years to establish the home. It was a team effort with the teams from Ohio and the Brazilian construction workers. They built an industrial-sized kitchen, as well as a large home with four suites, which would be used for the teen girls. They added on to the boys' house and the office buildings, and their last project was to build a perfect baby house that was named "Casa Esperança" or "House of Hope."

It was on one of these building trips that an unfortunate accident took place. When Dick and the team came to Brazil, they packed their suitcases with every type of tool from America that they might use. They had to do the hard work like laying cement blocks, sawing wood used to build the ceilings, and handling every kind of job, menial or large, to complete the building. It was during the sawing of the wood that Dick had an unfortunate accident. He cut his left hand very deeply between his first finger and his thumb. A woman who was working nearby looked at the gashing wound and very quickly got the first aid kit that was on the job site.

Dick's hand was professionally taped together; and to everyone's surprise, he said, "I have an appointment at Isa and Jeremy's school, where I will be giving a speech!"

I came to the project to pick up Dick and bring him to the school, where all the students were assembled in the big hall.

"Everything going okay at Lar Feliz?" I asked.

Dick was very quiet and simply said, "Yes."

When we arrived and Dick was speaking from the front, he was a little solemn and didn't seem like himself.

"As you are finishing your studies here in Brazil, college is definitely something to consider for your future if you don't want to wind up working at McDonald's," Dick said.

The students reacted with an open laugh at his honesty. They gave him a large applause, and they filed out of the auditorium and back to class.

Back in the car getting ready to return to Lar Feliz, Dick said to me, "I have had an accident and will need to go to a doctor shortly."

It was then that I noticed his hand and how it had been wrapped many times with white tape and gauze.

"We just happen to have a free clinic nearby," I said. I made a right turn in the little car, and we were there in only a few minutes.

The little hospital in Holambra looked old-fashioned to the eyes of someone so used to health care in North America. It had very good doctors, I had assured him; and it was run for free. Many times, workers and volunteers from Lar Feliz received help there.

"Is there anyone who can speak English?" Dick said as his eyes roamed around the waiting room full of young mothers and crying babies; wrinkled, little old ladies; and some youth who had a nasty cough.

We sat in the little white metal chairs for around an hour and a half after the nurse had taken Dick's name and his blood pressure.

"It shouldn't be much longer now," I said, attempting to be the voice of optimism.

At once, we were called to a tiny room inside the hospital where a male nurse spoke in broken English. He carefully removed Dick's bandages, cleansing the wound with a disinfectant.

"A surgeon is coming," he said as he motioned for Dick to sit on the table. "It will be a while," was all he said.

We sat in silence in the small clean room at the hospital, looking at the antiquated IV standing nearby.

"He should be back soon," I replied as I looked at my watch. We later learned that the surgeon was called away from his vacation to come and stitch up Dick's wounded hand.

"These hospitals are not the same as the American ones, but the people are friendly," he said, as a man with cowboy boots and hat entered the room and asked Dick some questions. He quietly asked how it had happened, and he cleaned and sterilized his hands and scissors.

"Is that the surgeon?" Dick said his thoughts out loud. Though he stayed quiet, his expression spoke for itself.

The well-trained surgeon quickly gave him an injection; and he went to work, stitching the wound back together. His nimble fingers gracefully executed the surgery with an uncommon skill. As quickly as it started, it was done; and with a slap on Dick's back, he wrote a prescription for an antibiotic.

"Have a nice visit in Brazil!" he said as he left the room.

After Dick had returned to America a week later, he went to his family doctor, who examined the stitches with an incredulous look on his face.

"Where did you say that you had this done?" he asked. "I have never seen anything like this! The surgeon did a beautiful job, and you probably won't even have a scar."

"Doctor, you wouldn't believe me if I told you," Dick said. "It was done in a little hospital in Holambra, Brazil.

The team gathered around at night and had meals together with Paul, Isa, Jeremy, and me. It was a time that everyone could talk about all the things that were troubling them to these matured saints from the home church in Ohio. Paul had expressed his desire to own a home in Holambra rather than pay rent, but it was nearly impossible for us to get a loan from a bank in Brazil with a decent interest rate.

"Come here, honey," Sandy said to me as she motioned for me to sit down.

We sat down to dinner with Sandy and Rich, Warren and Karen, and Dick. It was sloppy joes and salad—American food—with ice cream for dessert. We were each eating the fragrant ice cream that was so sweet. The taste was familiar, but what was it?

"Oh, Mom!" Jeremy said out of the blue. "It's corn-flavored ice cream!"

Everyone looked at each other with odd expressions on their faces, not knowing what to say next.

"Well, Sandy, was it on sale?" Warren asked with a puzzled look on his face. Everyone began to laugh hard because though people in Ohio loved to eat fresh sweet corn, it had never occurred to them to have it as a flavor of ice cream.

"Maybe next time, you should buy the lima bean flavored ice cream!" Warren said, and we laughed again.

Then, we sat down to play another game of cards. Hoots and hollers were heard from whoever won the hand at the time.

## CHAPTER 13
## *A Planting*

*"A house is made of walls and beams. A home is made of love and dreams."*

—Ralph Waldo Emerson

It was time for the team to go home; and after only a week and a half, much had been accomplished at Lar Feliz as well as in our own personal lives as a family. With the help of Dick, we were able to secure the loan from a bank in America to purchase our home in Holambra from a woman who lived in the Netherlands. "Complicated" was too small of a word for all the transactions that took place. Suddenly, the door was slammed shut with a large padlock on it and a thrown-away key.

"I will not sell the house!" said the elderly Dutch woman over the phone to Paul. "If you offer me whatever, I will still not sell it! The house is simply not for sale! I've changed my mind!" she said.

Paul quietly put down the phone with a stunned look on his face.

"She won't sell it," he said as he relayed the details to me.

"Why not?" I asked. There must be a reason. "Why let us hope for that after we have been living here so many months and fixing it up like it was our own?"

It seemed like a cruel joke, but it was true. For no reason that we knew of, the old Dutch woman who was our landlady, now living in the Netherlands, had made her final decision. The house, our dream home, was not for sale. We could continue renting it for as long as we wanted, or we could look further for a different house that we could buy. With the money of the loan in hand, we decided to do the latter.

We called a few different realtors and began the hunt for a new home with the financial loan from the US that we had secured. First, we looked at a small house without any garden at all that was painted top to bottom in mint green.

"I don't think it's for us," Paul told the woman helping us. "My wife likes to have a garden."

"Who needs to have a garden?" she asked with a laugh. "Then you have to work in it."

I just looked at Paul and shook my head. This was not the house for us!

We looked at huge houses, and we looked at small ones. None of them seemed right, until we came upon a house that was rather a fixer-upper. It was new, but it had never been finished right; and it had never been painted. The family, having gone through hard times, wanted to sell it fast for the right price. The cost was exactly the amount that we had on loan from the bank. It was a big house with lots of small compartments and rooms and an empty lot next door that could be turned into a beautiful garden. We signed on the line to buy the house, and we couldn't wait to get started.

We hit another bump in the road when the bank in Ohio delayed in sending the money to pay for the house that we had just purchased. As Paul prepared the check to pay the first of the two payments made to the bank, he got a knot in his stomach. Could God be trusted to do yet another miracle in this emergency?

At that time, a Canadian team came with Gordon and Bonnie to minister, and they began to hold a prayer meeting that the money would make it on time. Just like God always does, the money came right on time—not a day late and not a day early.

We had the house painted and put in a spiral staircase where the attic room would be the master bedroom. We talked long over what color to paint the outside of the house. The back veranda that was used to store shoes and bikes, we changed into an outside living room, where we could have big dinners and gatherings. For the garden, there was only a mango tree and a few palms, no grass or flowers and no green plants. It had pretty much been a place where the family before had dumped their trash and let their dogs run. Paul called a gardener who had been recommended, and he also found another who was a lot cheaper in price. The garden store that was well-known felt sure that they could turn the lot into a show-stopping garden, but their price was somewhat higher.

As with many other decisions, Paul, who lived off a gift income, made the decision based on the lowest price; though we knew the flower shop that was highly recommended and run by a Dutch family in Holambra, it was always a good idea to save a little money—or so we thought.

Monday morning came with golden sunlight, and the very friendly gardener came with his ideas and plans. He would move the small palm trees planted in the corner by the garden wall, and he would plant a large patch of deep green grass. Why, he would also plant a rose garden. "Only the best for the van Opstals," he had said.

*Always pay the workers of a product at the end of a completed task, including baking a cake, renovating a kitchen, painting a house, or planting a garden. Wise Brazilian advice we should have heeded.*

At the end of the week, the trees were transplanted; and the friendly gardener asked for the remaining money to be paid in advance so that he could shop for the roses over the weekend. Paul, who trusted just about anybody, reached out his hand and paid the large sum of money to the gardener in cash.

"See you on Monday!" he shouted as he drove away in his small truck.

On Monday, there was a gentle rain, which also appeared the following three days. Very little gardening could be done this week.

The next week, Paul called the number of the gardener. The phone rang and rang until the call reached the automatic answering service. Sadly, this went on for a few days. Was the gardener finished? Where was the grass and the roses? It seemed that he had forgotten a few things!

As foreigners in Brazil, we had, at times, been a target for salespeople who quoted higher prices for us than for Brazilians. We had experienced our share of being swindled, short-changed, and even insulted; but there was something about this loss of the long-desired garden of our own that added injury to the insult. At that moment, it would have been the most natural thing for us to have a negative world view toward the Brazilian people, but God had called us here. He was worthy of our trust. So, we waited for a reply from the friendly gardener.

The next week, a man who resembled our gardener rang the bell at the gate. We opened the door, and a man entered who was indeed the gardener's brother.

"I have been praying for him for many years," he said.

Paul nodded his head and showed understanding.

"I will contact him, and I will find out where he went," the brother said.

As it turned out, the gardener had gone to a faraway town on the beach, using our money to enjoy a get-away at a hotel.

The following week, the gardener came to the door with his hat in his hand, bowed head, and an apology on his tongue. His brother followed close behind him. He asked for more money to buy the grass that came in large rolls that were already pre-grown. Paul didn't want to trust this man, but he knew that he must trust God. The brother had asked for another chance, and Paul was willing to give it. By the end of the day, we had a beautiful yard with grass. It was complete but needed to be watered. It was a basic garden, and there wasn't enough money for roses.

"But later we could buy those ourselves," I said as Isa and Jeremy ran barefoot in the new grass.

We would make this a beautiful garden in time. God makes everything beautiful in the right time.[8] There were difficulties, but there was always something to be grateful for. God worked out everything for the best.

---

[8] Ecclesiastes 3:11

CHAPTER 14

# The Light at the End of the Tunnel

*"God setteth the solitary in families: He bringeth out those which are bound with chains: but the rebellious dwell in a dry land."*

Psalm 68:6

"My mother went away, and she never came home!" Andrea, a worker, sobbed the words out slowly as everyone sat in a circle during an in-house training time at Lar Feliz. I had known her as a dedicated worker who had a friendly smile and an even temper. She worked with children, but she initially had come to work with a disabled teenage boy who needed total care. After everyone had shared something in the group about their childhood memories, they all knew more about one another and how it had not been an easy road for most of the ones who sat there. The ones who had suffered the most regarding abandonment and poverty were those same ones who went out of their way to make the children feel at home at Lar Feliz with 100 percent dedication.

Our focus had been, for the most part, on the children and their varied needs; but what had been birthed in my heart was the need to reach out to these workers. These were Brazilians who were not only helpers in our vision, but they were also our friends; they were loved ones—practically like family!

Gui suffered from spinal meningitis as a toddler. He was unable to eat on his own, and he stayed in a wheelchair all his life of fifteen years. His mother had lovingly cared for him at home. But as he grew taller and his mother was aging, it became impossible for Gui to receive the care that he needed in his home. He arrived at Lar Feliz very thin and fragile. He had a rumbling cough that shook the room, and his whole body leaned to one side.

The day that he arrived at Lar Feliz was also the first day that Andrea came to work as his monitor and aide who would care for all his needs. A journal was kept each day of any changes or developments in his health. He was immediately loved by all the workers, and they went to great lengths to care for him and help him to develop and grow healthy and stronger. Gui had a special private room that was kept strenuously clean from all dust to protect him from any infection. Though he had his own private room to sleep and dress, he was not kept separate from the other children nor activities. Off he would go in his wheelchair with a staff person to the dining hall down below where he participated in Christmas parties, dinners, and other fun things. When the children were painting pictures, he was handed a paintbrush as well, though at times it fell to the ground after being loosed from his grip and soiled his t-shirt on its way down.

Though Gui could not communicate with words, the children always knew how he was or what he wanted to say.

"Today, Gui is sad. See?" a little curly haired girl said softly.

"How do you know?" I asked as I looked carefully to see what it was the little girl had noticed. Then looking at his face, I saw tears in the corner of his eyes, though he was expressionless.

Gui continued to grow well into his teen years, his frail, crumpled body developing into a young man of seventeen years. His helpless body was lovingly bathed and cared for as if he were a newborn baby. He continued to live, though his life expectancy was not for very long. He ate and drank and was alert, though his cough drained his strength. His lungs had suffered, and he shook as he gasped for air.

Christmas time came to Lar Feliz, and strings of simple white lights were hung on the veranda. It was Gui's favorite place to sit, and he stared into the lights for hours. It was his favorite way to pass the time.

On a certain night in December, Andrea was his monitor and was caring for him. He seemed so good and happy one evening as he watched the Christmas lights. She wrote, "I have never seen Gui so happy this evening. It seems like nothing can take the smile from his tired face."

That evening, Gui's heartbeat slowed and, eventually, came to a stop. Every attempt was made to revive him in the ambulance and the hospital. All of Lar Feliz and his family mourned, though they knew and understood that he had lived longer than the expectations of the medical staff. Before Gui went to his Heavenly home, he taught the workers of Lar Feliz many things. He taught them to believe in the beauty of the light during dark and helpless times. He expressed himself without words and was completely understood by a child who was the wisest of us all. He participated and enjoyed the activities of the majority, though he was limited in his frail body. He loved others; and they, in turn, felt and reciprocated his love.

At his funeral, there were tears. The medical staff at the nearby hospital praised the good work done by our staff—after all, Gui had experienced a good quality of life, even toward the end of his days. He was never forgotten. His time on earth was short and filled with trouble, as well as peace and love from those who were near. He came out of darkness into God's marvelous light. Now he was free to soar and run through a grassy field. I can just hear him laughing and shouting to his whole heart's content at home in Heaven.

## CHAPTER 15
# Love Knows No Bounds

*"Love begins at home."*[9]

—Mother Teresa

There once was a small, blonde Dutch woman from Holambra named Veroni. She had the tenacity of a freight train; and no matter how high the mountain, like those trains, she just kept going! Her love of social work brought her to visit Lar Feliz, where she fell in love with the workers and children alike, and she was a constant stream of encouragement in the desert of difficulty. It didn't matter about the problem that came with the child; she had some pretty good ideas to help. She made childcare fun as it was meant to be. After all, if the workers were having fun, so would the children. If the workers suffered in drudgery, often the children would also be unhappy, sad, and misbehave as a result. When they were having fun, they felt loved and connected with the adults in charge; there never were any problems at all; and they did exactly what they were told.

There once was a small family living in a dangerous neighborhood. They lived in a tiny home with four children and a mother. They didn't have a yard to play in; so as was custom in Brazil, they sat outside by the road watching

---

9 Mother Teresa, "Love Begins at Home" (Nobel Peace Prize acceptance speech, Oslo, Norway, December 11, 1979).

the people go by. The fair-haired children with curls and green eyes were beautiful and carefree until one fateful day.

A car was pulling out of the road with some young men who were gang members. The man in the passenger's side waved a loaded pistol in his hand as he was talking to the driver. As they sped down the road, they turned into the lane where the little family was sitting outside in the sun watching the world go by.

Suddenly, the gun went off without the gunman's knowledge until he turned and investigated the street, looking at the little family.

"Go! Go!" he shouted.

Without any courage, they sped away. The little family was left with a horrific turn of events. Their lives would never be the same. Each one would forever be changed.

To their horror, the family found that the oldest little boy, who was three years old, had a profusely bleeding head wound. His eyes were lifeless, but he was still breathing. He was rushed to the primitive hospital post in town, but then he was brought to the larger hospital in the city. He would live, but he would live a different life than the one that had been imagined before the careless accident.

Some years later, he and his younger sister moved to Lar Feliz. The tree of support by the immediate family had cracked and splintered under the weight of the new normal that now took place every day. The siblings were situated in the baby and toddler house because even though the boy had grown, he was using diapers and was unable to talk. The little sister was very frightened and angry at first. They didn't understand why they had moved; they didn't understand why many of the things happened to them that did, but they understood love when they saw it and experienced it. The little girl grew more beautiful every day, and she laughed and played with the workers and the children.

On one such day, Veroni came to visit Lar Feliz, as she often did, bringing gifts of help, toys, and boxes of candy. When she saw the young boy in the overcrowded baby house, she created a play space with wooden panels where the boy could crawl around freely. At that time at Lar Feliz, there were plans to build a bigger, more spacious house for the babies and toddlers; but until it was completed, they did what they could to care for the babies. They took them for walks and played on some swings that were nearby. They read books, played in the sand, and ate their meals together in the crowded little kitchen.

Veroni came often; and as she spent time with the boy, he smiled at her and learned to give hugs. It was at that time that she began to explore the possibility of adopting him, and she and her husband did just that. It all came together in a year or so, and John, the boy, did well. He grew tall and was able to learn to walk a few steps on his own. Veroni organized many fulfilling activities for him like horseback riding and swimming. He laughed and smiled often, giving hugs to all those he knew.

He is loved and cherished by many, and his years are filled with joy and goodness. His little sister grew like a rose and was adopted by the very first family that came to visit. She became like a princess, and she learned to dance and study at school; her life was totally altered from what it had been that fateful day on the sidewalk in front of their house.

## CHAPTER 16
# A New Life

*"And my spirit hath rejoiced in God my Saviour. For He hath regarded the low estate of His handmaiden: for, behold, from henceforth all generations shall call me blessed."*

Luke 1:47-48

Maria was a woman who was short in stature, but she made up for it in her physical and emotional strength. She worked alongside her husband at the flower farms in Holambra, a Dutch town with farmland founded after World War II. It was there that many of her family members came after her, also looking for a job that paid decent money. It was backbreaking work—sometimes in the blistering, hot sun. The straw hats that they wore helped a little, providing shade, though the sweat coming from the brow rolled all the way down to the crevice in one's neck. Long-sleeved shirts and long pants also did nothing for the ventilation of the body. The workers walked all day until their feet were numb at night.

One woman, a friend of mine, said that after working in the flower business, she was so sick of flowers that she couldn't stand the sight of them anymore. She sure didn't want any as a present. Chocolate—or anything, for that matter—was a welcome gift, but not flowers!

In the hot climate of Brazil, roses are grown during two seasons. They are cut and sold mostly in the flower stores in downtown Holambra, where tourists from all over Brazil would come to buy them after they had tasted the Dutch cuisine in the nearby restaurants. The fields of roses hold many colors and fragrances. Red, the most common color, is the symbol and remembrance of passionate love. Equally beautiful with a sweet scent are the pink and lavender tones of roses, which symbolize youth and modesty. The yellow and orange roses are a spectacle of grandeur symbolizing royalty, and white roses symbolized loyalty.

Maria had a large family with her husband, whom she loved. They were good Catholics, and they brought up their children with wisdom as well as love. The days working on the flower farm turned into months and then years, until one sad day, Maria's husband passed away while he was working in the field.

As Maria removed her heavy gloves to wipe the tears rolling down her face, her hand squeezed a single rose that she had been carrying, the thorns leaving a mark and a drop of blood. Her world would be forever changed. Maybe truthfully, her life was now over. Her life as she knew it would be over; and though she couldn't see just around the bend, there was a promising future just ahead.

Down the dirt road a little way further toward Jaguariúna were two adjacent farms called Lar Feliz. She had heard that these farms were shelters for children coming out of high-risk situations. The children came with bruises, some seen and some on their souls. They came from broken backgrounds, where they were given a fresh new start. In place of growing flowers, Maria—and eventually some of her family—would be privileged to "grow" children with love and with discipline.

When she came for her interview with Pastor Paul, she spoke with a light in her eyes about her love of children and how she had raised her own. She had a basic education, not studying further at a university. She went to the school of experience, where she had high marks. While Pastor Paul listened, he looked at Maria, short in stature and soft spoken and offered her the position that was available in the boys' house. She would be a monitor or educator, and she would be caring for the little boys' needs as well as teaching them many things.

The little boys came from all kinds of terrible situations. Maria prepared their breakfast of warm chocolate milk with French bread and butter. She watched and listened to them. She let boys be boys, in that they could play, ride bikes, yell, and run. She also taught them to sweep the floor, put away their dishes, and wash their cups after they drank. She helped them solve arguments, an endless task most days. She helped little boys throughout the years, never complaining once about a child and never giving up on a child. She continued to work for sixteen years at Lar Feliz.

One day, a child came who would tell his story without spoken words. His name was Amos, and his first impression of the farm was that of fear. He came from a far-away town called Nazare. Worship was happening in the main hall when he entered, accompanied by an adult. His eyes were wide with terror, but out of his mouth came only moans mixed with his tears. He shivered all over and ran back to the sleeping quarters alone. When Maria tapped on his shoulder, he looked but said not a word.

"I know. I know, it's hard," said Maria as she gently touched his arm.

"No one will hurt you here!" Maria turned to see the social worker nearby who would later tell the team the background for the new eight-year-old boy.

We learned that Amos was abused by his father, and it usually took place in the bathroom. Though Amos looked strong and healthy, he had terrible scars on the inside because of the traumas that he had experienced at home. He had irrational fears of any adults; and he never spoke, not even a word. When a man came in the room, he normally cowered and cried to himself. If he felt threatened by any of the other little boys, he would hit back.

Gradually, he fell into line with the rest of the little boys. For the first time, he could celebrate Christmas; and he received presents and a white chocolate cake for his birthday. He played with little cars around the house. He learned to pick mangos from the tree and ride a bike. Little by little, he said a few words.

"Thank you," Amos said one day with a small smile and a downward-tilted head. He took a piece of raisin bread from Maria's tanned weathered hand.

"You are welcome, my dear!" Maria said as she straightened her glasses, her eyes beginning to water.

The farm and the work of the land was always managed by a small team of men. They were excellent gardeners who knew all the secrets of the plants and trees. They knew when to plant; they knew when to trim; and they knew when to cut something down completely. A family of caretakers arrived—Pastor Celino with his wife, Lurdes—who grew a row of pretty flowers along the front of their house. Celino, a pastor of a small church in town, was also a man of prayer. He took care of all the animals that were still located at the farm. He knew about horses, and he enjoyed taking the little ones on buggy rides on a clear sunny day.

When he heard about a new child coming in, bringing with her the sad stories of her past, he would shake his head and cry out to the Lord. His face would have a shadow of sadness; but he would take his heavy heart to the Lord, and he and his wife would pray for each child. He prayed for every little brother and sister, for adoptions to go smoothly, and for little souls to be healed. He loved farming the land, and he loved those children.

During the rainy season, some of the boys came from the project to give some extra help. The idea was that the boys would learn the value of working the land; and at the same time, they would be a great help to Pastor Celino. One of the boys who came to work was Amos.

In the morning Amos came to work the land with Pastor Celino. In Brazil, it is always polite to greet one another with "hello" or "good morning"; but when Celino said, "Good morning" to Amos, he gave no reply but looked away quickly.

"Everything good?" Celino would ask, but Amos wouldn't answer.

Pastor Celino and I hoped that the quiet, fresh air of the fields would cause a calm to settle over the boy's heart and mind; so we encouraged Amos to go work whenever possible.

With time and patience, Pastor Celino began to gain Amos' trust. Slowly, they would exchange small sentences back and forth; and before long, Amos was talking more to Pastor Celino than he ever had to anyone else. He asked questions about the animals on the farm; he noted a particularly beautiful sunrise; and Pastor Celino told me he even asked for a second cup of milk one morning.

His recovery and his improvement were nothing short of a miracle; and through the months, he grew and played and became just like all the other little boys. He talked, laughed, and even yelled. Then came the sad and happy day, the bittersweet moment when he would say goodbye to Lar Feliz. After a careful study of his family had been done, it was discovered that he had an older sister who loved him and would take care of him in her home with her family. He would go on a short holiday to her home in Nazare.

Pastor Celino came to wish Amos a wonderful time with his family and gave him a hug. With his face toward the back, Amos could not see the tear-filled eyes hidden behind the cheerful goodbye.

"Bye!" Amos said as he skipped away to the car. "I'll see you in a month!" and he gave a happy wave.

Things worked out for the better for Amos, and he never returned to Lar Feliz. Though Pastor Celino was unusually sad the day he waved goodbye to Amos—as were all the staff—we knew in our hearts that we could rejoice knowing that this was for the best. Amos was better now; he was healed and ready to be with a new family. He would have a home, a place of his own where he would grow up and be cared for by his loving sister.

While we were so impressed with the work of Maria at the little boys' house, we were also impressed with her daughter, Jane, who came soon after during the beginning years of Lar Feliz. She worked with the same quiet voice of authority and a hand of love.

She loved all the children, from the sick babies who came in the night to the rebellious teenage girls in their skimpy halter tops and the little boys playing marbles in the sand in front of the house. Through the years, Lar Feliz became like her home; she worked so many long hours. Adults and children liked her the same. She was kind, and she was fair.

When I asked Jane which of the children left the biggest mark, she told me that it was the little baby named Luke.

I was in charge of the baby house at the time when one day, a beautiful, young, dark-skinned pregnant girl came to Lar Feliz just before her baby was due to be born. Working with pregnant teenagers for the most part was very tricky. She had been using drugs, and she was brought for the baby's health and protection. She had some months to go, and I tried my best to get to know her a little bit. We were always encouraged to help the teen mothers take care of their own babies. I learned through experience that I couldn't teach them, no matter how much I wanted to, to love their babies. There were very young girls who, in spite of everything, would love their babies and take them home. Then there were young girls who would give their beautiful babies up for adoption to go to another loving family.

When the time came for the baby to be born, Jane took the girl to the hospital and attended the delivery. A new baby boy was born, and he was named Luke. Mother and baby were both fine. When the baby arrived back at Lar Feliz, we noticed that he was blond. How was it possible this little blond cherub was the son of the dark young woman? It was possible; and it happened more often in Brazil where interracial marriage was not only accepted, it was celebrated. He was beautiful.

"Do you think he will get any darker as he gets older?" the young mother asked.

We didn't know for sure. "Maybe," we said trying to reassure her.

The baby grew into a handsome toddler with dark ringlets of hair, which framed his pale-skinned face. He laughed when we tickled his belly, and he smiled almost all the time. His attachment to Jane seemed to grow when she brought him home sometimes on the weekend if he was sick or he needed to have a special doctor's appointment. He was an adorable little soul who appeared nothing at all like his mother.

His mother experienced youthful rebellion in all its forms. Sadly, those maternal feelings just never came; and she lacked any interest in her child. One night, she and another teen mother ran away, leaving baby Luke behind. She never returned. She didn't seem to be a fit mother, even when she tried to be; and one day, she realized that she didn't want her baby anymore. She called the social worker and signed the release form for adoption. It was for the best.

It seemed the mother didn't even give it a second thought. Perhaps she only thought of her coming freedom—freedom from responsibility and freedom to be on her own without a care in the world.

This was a difficult time for Jane, emotionally. I knew the bond she had formed with the little baby whose mother thought was too blond. With each passing day, the reality that baby Luke would soon leave us became clearer. Once he was adopted, we knew that we would likely never see him again; and this reality affected us all deeply—especially Jane.

The week finally arrived when a pair of prospective parents came for a visit. It was no surprise to anyone that they fell in love with the baby boy. It had been "love at first sight." It would be time for him to leave soon, and we began to gather the little baby's things. Though he had come to Lar Feliz with only one outfit, he would leave our home richer with a handmade quilt, a few pairs of shoes, some outfits and pajamas, some toys, and a package of diapers. Everything was ready, and we prepared our hearts to say goodbye. Jane was called away at a school meeting.

When she arrived back, she was cheated of her goodbye to the baby boy. She found a few coworkers in tears in the storage room. Happy tears mixed with sad were flowing. Saying goodbye was the hardest day when working at the baby house. Jane was sad to see that he was already gone. Life has a way of tricking our hearts sometimes, and who could understand it?

It took her a long time to forget about the little baby. She wondered where he had gone; and most importantly, she wondered if he was happy with his new mom and dad.

Jane later told me that one day in the grocery store, she heard a voice in the very town where she lived.

"Luke!" It was the name that had been given to the baby boy. It was not a very common a name in Brazil.

When Jane turned around to see, she discovered that it was him, holding the hand of his mother. He had a smile on his lips and a carefree laugh. He had grown.

"They looked happy," she told me with fresh tears running down her face.

It had been the perfect ending to a busy day when God allowed Jane to see that all was well. It was a comfort to know God was taking care of everything.

## CHAPTER 17
# Sitting At the Table

*"The table is a meeting place, a gathering ground,
the source of sustenance and nourishment, festivity, safety, and satisfaction."*[10]

—Laurie Colwin

At the baby house, or Casa Esperança, a large, round wooden table was custom made to accommodate a big group of children with a few adults. The wooden chairs were made a little bit higher for a small child to reach the table to eat.

At this big, round table, many extraordinary things took place daily. A prayer was uttered before the midday meal. Songs were sung, and games were played. Also, "knutselen" took place, which is the Dutch word for tinkering or doing arts and crafts. The large table became an almost sacred place where many memories were made.

When small children arrived at Lar Feliz, they were recovering from extreme trauma; and more than likely, they had difficulties with lack of appetite, trouble sleeping at night, and bed-wetting. Every day, the children at Lar Feliz were served a healthy, delicious home-cooked meal. Before coming to the home, many of the children were malnourished. Sometimes, they survived only on bags of chips and meager portions of noodles or rice. For

---
10  Laurie Colwin, *Home Cooking: A Writer in the Kitchen* (New York: Vintage, 2010).

this reason, it was of the utmost importance to make mealtime a happy time. It is not possible or recommendable to force a child to eat when they don't have the desire to do so.

For breakfast, they ate fresh buns with warm milk. Every other meal consisted of the Brazilian rice and beans, some meat, and a small salad or vegetable mixture.

Making rice and beans just right took a lot of practice; but once mastered, the taste and the combination of the Brazilian rice and beans is healthy and unforgettable.

Many lovely moments took place around the table at Lar Feliz. There were women's meetings on International Women's Day at which each woman was encouraged in her work with the children at the project.

With most of the staff being women, I would often say, "Without God, Lar Feliz would not exist; but without women, Lar Feliz would also not exist!" The women would giggle and humbly look down, though they knew it to be true.

Paul would say, "But you are not getting a raise!" Everyone would laugh hard. Paul seemed to get away with making all kinds of jokes without losing his authority as a boss.

At the long tables in the dining room, there were Christmas parties complete with Santa and presents for the children. There were also birthday parties for children and adults alike. There, we held meetings, training sessions, and fed many teams that came through from other lands, like Canada, the United States, the Netherlands, and even South Africa. There were worship times together with flowing, jazzy music which filled up the property.

Many people came and went over the years. People came who seemed like they would be friends forever; but after returning home, we rarely heard from them again. Paul and I hosted a myriad of people, and we were enriched and blessed for the most part; but we were also blessed by the Brazilian people who stayed rather than went back home.

It was not unusual for visitors to come by throughout the day. Sometimes, during the holidays, chocolates or gift-wrapped toys were brought. One sunny day at the baby house, as the monitors and I were sitting and having lunch, a tall girl and boy who appeared to be brother and sister walked briskly—half-running, half-walking—to the play area outside our house; and it seemed that they knew the way. They turned into the house and came close to the table. They were dressed in the finest name-brand clothes, and their dark brown skin was glistening with health and beauty. They were both tall for their age, and their hair was styled with the latest haircut.

"Hello, Tía Jill!" they said politely. They had remembered me; but at first, I couldn't remember where I knew them from. They held out their hands, and their beautiful smiles revealed perfect bright white teeth.

"Why it is Patricia and Rafael!" I said with excitement. The monitors erupted in laughter as did the two children. Smiles and hugs followed. They were okay! They were more than okay; they were fabulous! A new home had done miracles in their lives. Their new mama had loved them well. They were made new, and we hardly recognized them. I remembered back to when I met their mom—a drug addict who had decided to give them up for adoption. I also remembered how the first couple who came to meet the siblings quickly refused the adoption without getting to know them. We prayed as a staff for the right parents, and God answered. Their radiance helped me to see the fruits of all of our prayers and hard work, and it was delicious.

While Patricia had lived at Lar Feliz, one of the monitors had braided her African hair into a weave. The little one would sit for hours in the monitor's lap until her long braided hairstyle was complete. Now she wore her hair in a short, straight look that was in fashion.

"Yes, Tía, it's us," they said together. "Can we play in the park where we used to play?"

"Why, sure you can! Do you want to eat with us?" I asked.

"No, thank you, we are not hungry. We just wanted to play on the slide where we used to play and to see where we used to live."

They ran through the kitchen to the little park that was an outdoor playroom for the babies and toddlers, complete with bikes, swings, a small garden and sandbox, and a little wooden house with a sliding board. They played until the place that they longed for had satisfied their hearts, and then their beautiful mama told them it was time to go home.

Adoption for the small children from the baby house inevitably was a very happy ending. They were able to experience a loving home, most of the time with two parents as well as grandparents, uncles, aunts, and cousins which make a child feel complete—no longer abandoned or orphaned. Couples from all walks of life came with eager, open hearts to adopt children in Brazil—a country that loves its children.

"It's story time!" I spoke. The small children gathered around me at the table. There were ten in total with a set of twins, eagerly listening.

"There once was a house filled with princes and princesses."

"Princesses?" exclaimed one little girl with warm brown eyes.

"Yes, they all lived in a little house together. They played in the grass, and they had rice and beans to eat and wonderful soups during the wintertime. They learned many things: how to behave, how to be polite, and how to pick up their toys at night. Most importantly, they learned how to love and to be kind."

"They learned how to respect!" one of the other monitors entered the story, giving her advice.

"Then one day, a beautiful mama and papa came to take them to their new home. They had a new bed for them with new clothes, and they would make some new memories. And that is the end of the wonderful story, and it is a true story!"

The little children looked on with satisfied faces as they realized that they were a part of such a wonderful story. They held hands and said a prayer before eating their lunch of rice, beans, salad, and meat. They smiled as they dreamed of tomorrow.

When we were first living in Brazil, it took me quite a few tries to learn how to make rice and beans which is the most important part of the Brazilian's diet. I had to learn to use a pressure cooker. I burned a few pans black on the bottom, and I had to endure dry tasteless white rice until I finally learned the secrets from the Brazilian women. Everything starts with oil, garlic, and a tiny bit of onion. Measurements are flexible, just remember to use two parts water to one part rice. Brazilians do not function well without their rice and beans. They complain of feeling sick and weak. After changing to the Brazilian diet, I never had trouble with anemia again, which was something that I had for many years. Rice and beans with meat and salad is a diet that I would recommend to anyone.

## CHAPTER 18
# A Lost Brother and Sister

*"And whosoever shall give to drink unto one of these little ones a cup of cold water only in the name of a disciple, verily I say unto you, he shall in no wise lose his reward."*

Matthew 10:42

A brother and sister, Davy and Mary, arrived at Lar Feliz in the early hours of the morning. Their sweet smiles melted the tender hearts of all the women staff at the baby house. They came, bringing only what they were wearing, with a hunger and a thirst for love. That evening, Paul told me the story of Davy and Mary, who resembled a modern-day Hansel and Gretel lost in the woods.

The brother and sister were loved by a mother who was alone. One day, she met a man who wanted nothing to do with her children from her previous relationship. She must choose! She could accept the conditions of her new live-in-boyfriend and be with him but without her children, or she could keep her children and never see her boyfriend again. She bathed them and clothed them nicely; and taking their hands, she decided to take them to the child protection office for the social worker to find them a new home—much like lost puppies.

The social worker rejected her case, so the lonely mother took the hands of her children and led them out the door. She was still unsure of what to do when she suddenly had a thought! She made her decision. The brother and sister were left on the streets of a nearby town to fend for themselves. They went for days, which turned into weeks, without any real food. The hard-hearted mother coldly turned her back on their cries as she began her new romance with the man of her dreams. She would be taken care of, and she would be given affection and new clothes in return for the horrible neglect of her two small children who wandered aimlessly around the town by themselves. They were picked up off the streets by a child worker who brought them to Lar Feliz after some calls and paperwork.

They were naturally beautiful with ringlets of gold and light brown hair on their heads. Davy had green eyes and looked like a cherubim angel, and so he was called Angel by the women who worked at the children's home. It didn't take long, however, before he was into much mischief like throwing toys and fighting with the others—so much so that the women there considered giving him a new nickname!

Davy and Mary were having trouble in bed-wetting and not being able to eat or sleep. When Mary sat down to eat, she ate one or two bites; and afterward, she couldn't eat any more. No amount of pleading or coaxing by the staff would help her to eat more.

"Eat your tomatoes, and you will have rosy cheeks!" the day monitor said.

"Rice and beans will make you strong like Tía Selma!"

"Have some meat, and your hair will be curly!" the women said to the children one after another, but it was of no use. Mary refused to eat and only stared at her plate. Everything was tried, including putting small portions on her plate. Mary ate a little but never enough.

Davy constantly wet his pants and bed, and he also couldn't play properly with the other children there.

"Play together!" the teacher exclaimed as she saw Davy grab the new green ball and make a run for it. A fight between the boys was almost always about to explode.

"Throw the ball back and forth," the monitor said. "See! It's like playing catch!"

Two of the monitors threw the ball back and forth between each other so that the children got the idea. It took a while; but finally, they learned.

I had a schedule that included nature walks, games, painting, and play dough; and these different activities seemed to help calm the children so that, over time, they healed and were able to function at a normal level.

It was a joy and, at times, a challenge to find and discover activities that would soothe and relax a child from stress as well as help them to have fun and play—one of the most important activities of childhood. As they walked along the paths on the edge of the woods by the lake, the quiet breath of the child settled into a contented rhythm. As they watched the animals and the birds, their anger and agitation melted away amid the nature. Coloring and playing with playdough also had a therapeutic result.

We often took the children along a path in the wooded jungle area where we came to the farm that had some animals. The children loved to help feed the chickens, and there was even horse riding arranged where they could ride on horseback or in a buggy together with me. The fights and the tension filtered away as they saw a hummingbird come near the water where they walked. It was a magical moment walking together on the spacious land at the adjoining farms.

The fresh air of the jungle enveloped us as we noticed the tiny masterpieces of nature. The children and I often picked wildflowers along the way to make bouquets for the women working back at the house. Pastel butterflies flitted by with the occasional blue morpho that stole the show—its iridescent color shimmering in the sunlight. Every eye and attention span were locked in. Small children's hands tried to reach him and bring him home alive. There is a fable that those blue butterflies bring good luck and fortune.

"If one happens to land on you, expect some new beginning to happen in your life," I was told by a Brazilian.

I was holding Davy in my arms as we walked back home. He pointed to a place at an open field, and said, "There is my mother! She is over there! Do you see her?" He pointed frantically over to the open field, as he tried to get me to see what he was seeing. Many times, when he talked to me, it was only gibberish; but this time, it was clear, though I didn't know what it was that he meant.

"No, she's not there!" I said shaking my head. As I peered over at the field, I didn't see anyone.

A week later, a social worker arrived with some shocking news.

"We have some very important news! The mother of Davy and Mary has suddenly died!"

"What do you mean?" the psychologist said.

"She was murdered with a knife through her heart!" the social worker said.

"You have got to be kidding!" Pastor Paul said in disbelief.

"The police believe that her live-in boyfriend stabbed her through the heart with a knife. They searched the whole town but couldn't locate him. It seems that he is on the run."

"Now the children can go for adoption! They are free to have a new and better life," Pastor Paul stated directly.

A couple would come soon to meet them. Though difficult at first, the prospective parents would win over the hearts of the brother and sister. It was a sensitive situation that the couple would take on. If they showed affection too quickly, they might frighten the brother and sister away. The best way to begin the bond was slow and steady. It was a process that gave full respect to the feelings and desires of the children and prospective parents. Either party could stop the process at any time.

The first meeting went as expected. The children were a bit shy at first, but they sensed the love that was there.

When I came back to my work after a few days off, I hurriedly went down to the dining hall to see Davy in the strong arms of his new father, a big burly man with a contagious laugh. On Davy's little face, I saw a contented smile;

and his sister Mary was nearby with her new vivacious mother. It had all worked out, and a new family was born.

"Do you want a hug goodbye?" I asked shyly.

Davy shook his head. Maybe a handshake was better in the end. The children were getting a new dad and mom today. They would forget all about Lar Feliz and the workers and myself. They would have no memory of their time with us, but they would forever be imprinted on all our hearts; and if we did our job right, they would know that deep inside, they are loved.

CHAPTER 19
## True Love

*"Beareth all things, believeth all things, hopeth all things, endureth all things. Charity never faileth."*

1 Corinthians 13:7-8a

*The van Opstal family and Lar Feliz blog:*
*August 30, 2011*
*"The Trees of Love"*

*At the project, we have several large mulberry trees that are filled with berries. "Amora" is the Brazilian name for these tall gracious trees. "Amora" is a word very similar to "Amor," the word for love in Portuguese. At almost any time of day, one can see all the children of all ages, as well as adults, picking those berries off the trees.*

*Whenever a child is missing, we can usually find him picking berries— as much as he can eat. The babies and toddlers come to the trees at certain times of the day only to return with purple hands and covered from head to toe in the purple juice.*

*Like the berries on the trees, the children of Lar Feliz are looking for love. Many times, they know exactly where to find it, who has it, and who doesn't. They can tell right away when someone says that they love them, but they are false. Most of the children have been let down so many times that they are careful. Once they have found the person who truly loves them, they keep coming back to him or her again and again.*

I sat in the sitting room of the baby house—or House of Hope, as it was named. There had been a position open for a new monitor, and I needed to interview a few different women. As they talked about their education and work experience, I usually cut to the heart of the matter and asked them the most important question of all.

"Do you love children? I mean, really love children, not just like them enough to be able to get a job," I said with a certain clarity.

An attractive young woman gave a confident smile as she looked at her long copper-painted nails and uncrossed and recrossed her legs.

"Of course, I love children," she stated. "They are exactly what this world needs!"

I looked her over and considered. The woman was young and attractive, and it seemed that she was a regular church-goer.

"You start tomorrow night! Remember, with all children, you will have good days and bad days. If you really love them, that love will carry you through the bad days. Hopefully, there will be a lot of good days, though," I said as I went out the door to go home.

The next morning, when I arrived at the baby house, I heard that some of the children didn't like the new monitor, but they didn't say too much.

"That new monitor is ugly!" the little boy said and shook his head.

*What could it mean?* I thought.

The new monitor was pleasant and kind to the other women, but the children seemed to shy away from her. Maybe they just needed to get used to her. The woman cleaned the kitchen thoroughly and always had just the right words to say.

One morning, to my dismay, I arrived at work to find scratch marks on a little girl's arm.

The little girl, Amanda, had a stubborn streak; and she never wanted to go to bed at night. The red marks left on her arm were clearly made by someone with long nails grasping her arms tightly.

"What happened?" I questioned the new worker. I was distraught, and I found it hard to believe.

"I lost it when she wouldn't listen to me," she said slowly through her tears. "I guess this job wasn't right for me. I just don't have enough patience."

She left that day never to return.

> *Lar Feliz Blog*
> *August 26, 2012*
> *A New Family Arrives*
>
> *Two weeks ago, we received a request for help from a faraway town. Three hours away, there was a family of five children, who, after being removed from their home, were suffering neglect and lack of good care in the institution where they were placed because of the overcrowding of the former children's home. A visit from the city's social workers gave us the impression that our work was desperately needed to help children even in faraway towns. They said that our homes were "first world," which is a huge compliment from Brazilian authorities.*
>
> *The five children arrived; three would stay in the baby house, and a set of twin sisters would stay in the little girl's house. Their ages were one, three, five, and eight. The little baby girl had her first birthday on the date that they arrived at Lar Feliz. She is a content, smiling, sweet baby girl. The two middle boys had difficult names that even the Brazilians have trouble pronouncing. I repeated their names five times quietly to myself, a practice that I do to help me remember all the names of the children who come through.*

*The five-year-old boy saw all the toys and kept playing all day long, riding bikes and playing with little hot wheel cars. He seemed happy and was not difficult at all to lead. The other little boy, who is three, presented a problem that we all noticed immediately. When we talked to him, he gave no response. When asked a question, he didn't answer with questions or words. He also had tiny wounds on the inside of his ears. We wondered if it was an emotional problem or physical.*

*So, one of our workers made him an appointment with a specialist that she knew, and she took him there during her free time. We later discovered that in the past, he had an ear infection that left him partially deaf in one ear. The second or third day that I came in to work, he raised his arms for me to lift him up; and when I did, he gave me a huge smile. As he is growing accustomed to the baby house, he makes more sounds—like "varoom" when he is playing with the cars—and he cries now when he is upset. I was even surprised to hear from my workers that he quietly said my name when I arrived.*

*The five-year-old boy is always by my side, wanting to color and participate in any of the artistic activities that we do at the baby house. He is always smiling now, and he asks me to pray extra for him. He is very eager to start school. We discovered also that one of the twin sisters has a weak heart, which can be dangerous if left untreated. They are very happy to pass by Casa Esperança to see their siblings. It is situations like these that help me keep going, even when faced with challenges and opposition. It is for the children that Lar Feliz exists "because God loves the children" [our motto on our logo].*

A Volkswagen van that had come a long way, winding around the country dirt roads, brought a tearful couple to the baby house. They had recovered from drug addictions, and they came to visit their family of five small children. It had been a hard road in rehab, but every painful moment was worth it if they were able to get their children back again. The man was tall and handsome with dark hair combed over with sideburns. The woman was a petite blonde with an angelic-looking face. They seemed repentant for what they had done, and they were praying that they would get another chance to be a family again.

As they got out of the van, they were offered a small cup of coffee by the social worker at Lar Feliz. A little lower than humiliation they felt as they ventured over to the dining room to visit all five of their children who had been gathered. They were greeted by smiles and laughs all around; and they received joyful, tearful hugs. They held in their hands some simple gifts that had been wrapped in bright red paper. The woman opened a bag that contained some soda and a simple chocolate cake that had been recently baked and wrapped in tin foil. The children giggled with glee, and their one son who did not talk very much did a little dance as they opened the simple toys and the new shoes that had been bought. Because the children were so happy, I always enjoyed whenever the parents came; and it was beautiful to see the changes each time.

They would return the next week, and then the next—until after some months of good visits, the judge would hear their case to get their family back again.

Nothing would ever be the same as what it had been before; but with God's help, it would be even better.

After examining their progress in finding work and staying clean from drugs, the judge ruled that they were allowed to take their children home.

A house inspection was also carried out, which had revealed a simple home with enough room for the love and care of a growing family. It was a happy but sad day when the team and I said goodbye to the children to whom we had grown attached. When two adults succeeded in changing their situation for their children, that was a happy day to remember! They would all be together again.

For me, it was wonderful to hear the reaction of the children.

"Really, Mama? We are going home?" the oldest sister asked, hardly believing their ears.

"Yes, we are, dear one! Let's gather your things!"

They went into the girls' bedroom, where they found stacks of pink and yellow t-shirts, some matching shorts, and jeans. Each of the twins also brought four or five pairs of shoes.

At the baby house, there were large plastic bags of clothes, enough for the three youngest children. The monitors came out with big smiles shining through their tears, as they gave the very best for the children to take home. They also had a bike that they gave for the little boy to ride, and there was a wooden truck and some dolls, too.

The mom told us how grateful she was for everything that we did as the dad nodded his head in agreement.

"Come on home, kids!" the dad said as he scooped up the second son, whose face was shining with excitement.

They got their belongings and made their way over the hill to the office, where the social worker would explain everything to the parents about any medications or health issues that they would need to know about. A letter was given with their habits, likes, and dislikes—something written down that would make the road a little smoother going home. Precious information we passed on like the passing of the torch to ensure that quality care would continue in the years to come.

As they turned to leave in the Volkswagen van, the smallest son waved his hand furiously and said with a loud voice, "Goodbye, Lar Feliz!"

## CHAPTER 20
# A Dog's Day

*"The wolf and the lamb shall feed together..."*

Isaiah 65:25

As our family passed by another little hardware shop, I held my breath and stayed silent, wondering if Paul had noticed as we walked on. Yes, Paul had seen the shop, and all four of us went in on the humid afternoon.

In the front of the store, there were aquariums with all kinds of brightly colored fish. The strong smell of animal food took one's breath away as we continued to walk down the aisle which held cast iron cookware, leather work boots, plastic watering containers, shovels, and dish towels. Finally, we walked to the back of the store and saw an assortment of animals for sale. There was something for everyone here!

"Oh, how sweet!" Isa said as she wriggled her little hand into the cage to pet a black and white bunny. "Can I have one, Papa?"

"Uh, let me think about it. No!" Paul said briefly before Isa got too attached. "Do you know how messy the bunny cage will get? Are you willing to clean it? Well, I am not!"

We continued to the very back of the store, where we heard a rooster crow loudly. The cages diagonally across from the hens and peeps held a multitude of brightly colored parakeets for sale.

"How about a bird or two?" Paul suggested.

"No, thanks, but maybe I would like this little puppy!" said Jeremy, pointing us in the direction of a medium-sized poodle.

Paul relented, and we cuddled the new puppy in the back seat of the hot car as we made our way home. We named him Bruiser, and he fit right in with our three other dogs and a parrot that had an eerie laugh.

It certainly wasn't out of the ordinary that our family found stray animals to bring home. It happened on a regular basis. If our home became too full or completely chaotic because of our beloved pets, we would give a creature away to a worthy home. Having animals was a way for all of us to unwind and relax. It made our home an interesting and fun place to be.

Some happy and some sad things took place at our home with all the animals. It was also true that the pets that stayed on usually got along well with one another until one disastrous day when we adopted a beautiful German shepherd named Chivas.

Many robberies were taking place in the small town of Holambra. There were people that we knew of whose homes were being broken into. Even the gas station in the center of town fell victim. We grew afraid, and we felt vulnerable that maybe our house was the next on the list to be robbed! Isa and Jeremy had many of the American toys that were still very expensive in Brazil. We decided to get a trained watch dog that would protect our home. Chivas had been trained to attack intruders, and she was not a friendly, family dog. She stayed in her penned-up space during the day, and the idea was for her to be let loose at night to protect our home from unwanted intruders.

When any acquaintance came by for a visit, we would have to yell from outside the gate, "Amigo!" or our friends would be attacked and torn apart by Chivas (who was named after a popular beer in Brazil). Sometimes, I wondered if the trainers had drunk a bit too much of that beer while training her.

"We are home!" Jeremy yelled when we came in through the gate that led inside our house.

The watch dog, Chivas, was quiet in the front yard. The gate was shut but failed to clasp and lock completely. Janke, our little miniature pincher, or "minpin" for short, was a fierce and feisty personality inside a small body. She barked and growled in a way that gave a warning, even though her size was small. She always slept with the children and watched over them. She was precious to them.

"Janke, Janke!" I called. It was a bright sunny day, and Janke pranced out to the front of the veranda to get some sun.

At that horrible moment, Chivas charged out of her pen, heading straight for little Janke laying in the sun.

"No! No!" I heard myself scream.

It was like a bad dream. Chivas bit little Janke's body in the middle with her jaws, and she began to shake Janke like a ragdoll.

"I said no!" I yelled again; and without a thought, I grabbed Janke from Chivas the attack dog. Janke was still alive; but she was bleeding profusely, and her breath was coming and going out in short segments. Was it too late to save her?

Paul came home from the project to find Jeremy and me crying, holding our little dog one last time. He quickly got Chivas back into her pen; and without hesitation, he brought Jeremy with Janke in his arms down the road to the family vet named Renato.

When they arrived, Renato, with his eyes full of doubt, looked down at the table as the life of Janke started to fade. There was nothing that could be done. Surgery would not help her internal injuries, and she would have to be put down. Isa was called from her friend's house, where they were working on a school project, to say goodbye over the phone.

Janke died a hero. She was a small, feisty dog who faced off with another giant dog to protect her family. When everything was said and done, the van Opstal family took a vote to see if we should keep Chivas even after what had happened. The vote was three to one—the one vote being Paul. The kids and

I voted against keeping her. The next day, Chivas was taken away and went back to her trainer. We didn't even say goodbye.

Once Chivas was gone, it took some time to forget all the images in our minds—images of Janke standing strong against a mean and vicious dog who was ten times her size. She laid down her life for her family. It would be the last mean watchdog that we would ever own.

As for the other dogs, there were many along with cats, birds, hamsters, bunnies, and a rat named Zelda. They gave our family many happy memories, bringing joy and laughter to our home.

After visiting our uncle Bud one day in Wooster, Ohio, our family fell in love with his Golden Retriever named Charlie. After one of our Boxers had passed away, it was decided that our family would adopt a four-month-old Golden, whom we proudly named Charlie. He was a gentle, old soul, even while he was still a pup. He was well behaved and loved to have his neck stroked. He loved children and adults alike.

He had been the life of the party for Jeremy's birthday. The little boys were invited to a slumber party at our house. In the office, the boys had their computers and played their games into the night. Only Charlie was invited into the room with them, where they had a feast of mini pizzas and birthday cake.

"Hey, Charlie, do you want some birthday cake and soda?" asked one of the boys.

"He likes it!" the boys said and nodded all around. The doors were closed, so Paul and I couldn't see what was going on.

Paul and I were watching a film on the couch when suddenly groans and screams erupted from behind the closed office door.

"Oh no, Charlie threw up! Gross!" they cried.

"I'll go and clean it up," said Paul.

One by one, the little boys ran out of the room like they had partaken in a horror movie. It wasn't the first mess that Paul had cleaned, and it wouldn't be the last! Charlie was the life of the party, a favorite among children and adults wherever he went.

We also owned another Boxer—a brindle named Duke. He was an ornery pup, who dug out all my roses. If I planted a rose bush and it started to bloom, the next day it would be gone as Duke would eat the fragrant flower in one gulp. It was probably because he loved the sweet smell of them. He got himself into lots of trouble, but he was also quite comical. One day, when we took the children from Lar Feliz to the zoo, Jeremy was left at home to watch over Duke and the house. Charlie was like a big brother to Duke, who loved to whine, play, and sing to the tune of a harmonica.

When Paul and I got home from the zoo—an all-day trip—we were surprised to look out into our yard and find all different types of food items. There were packages of macaroni noodles that had been opened and spread out in the grass, some opened packages of coffee that gave off a rich fragrance, and a carton or two of milk that had been chewed open and spilled out on the hot concrete.

*What on earth is going on?*

We came into the house to find Jeremy with his headphones on, playing computer games and oblivious to all that had happened that day.

"Jeremy!" Paul yelled. "What is going on? You were supposed to be watching the dogs!" Charlie winked and wagged his tail as if he were the innocent one.

"Come on, everybody! Let's clean up this mess," I said.

"How am I supposed to get these pasta noodles off of the lawn?" Jeremy asked.

"Why not try a rake?" Paul suggested, and it worked!

Duke grew older, and he made the van Opstal family smile quite a few more times until he suddenly grew ill from cancer and passed away. It took a while for us to forget the pain of losing a pet. After all, they were like our family! Usually, when we bought a new dog, we were able to forget the pain of loss. That was the only thing that seemed to do the trick.

There were also dogs at the children's home who were great watchdogs and good company. Tessa and Agape were two nice German Shepherds who were trained to fetch little stones that were thrown out into the field, instead of a ball.

"Well, I have never seen dogs play fetch with rocks before!" Mother Baughman, my mom, said when she came to visit our family in Brazil.

"We don't have any dog toys here at the farm, and we make do with what we have!"

"A nicer, more attentive watchdog is hard to find! Tessa and Agape are special dogs."

Animals were a strong element of life for us while living in a foreign country. They were part of our family, providing protection and blessing us with special memories.

CHAPTER 21

# Child's Play is Divine

*"When a child is at play, he nourishes his soul."*[11]

—Vera Alves

## Doylestown, Ohio
1978

The sun was shining with a faint breeze blowing through the weeping willow tree. The long, sinewy ropes were tied to a knotted branch that dipped below the others and was adjacent to the house. Lynnie and I took turns swinging high on the homemade swing at our grandparents' farm. We walked through fields of wild buttercups to the old barn where we came to a nest of kittens in the straw. The mama cat was black with orange patches and wild green eyes. She was feral. Time and again, she hid her beautiful bundle of kittens in a different corner of the barn.

Lynnie and I would carefully find them on Sunday afternoons. We would hold the kittens as they got older, taming them as we looked into their small eyes. Out of the batch, there was a male who was completely orange with stripes like a tiger.

---

11   Vera Alvez, "The Importance of Play" (Enrichment course, Lar Feliz, Jaguariúna, Brazil, 2011).

"Mom and Dad told me I could have one! I think I will take this one. Isn't he pretty?" I whispered to my cousin Lynn.

"Yes, he is," said Lynn.

After a few more weeks, we brought him home.

"What is a good name?" I asked.

"How about Catfish?" my brother, Jason, asked. He had just been fishing with Dad and was fascinated by it.

"Catfish it is," I said with a nod.

For me and the other grandchildren, it seemed that all heavenly gifts came from our grandparents' farm. Beside the house were about six lilac bushes that grew together forming one big clump, and they smelled delicious in the summertime when the windows were left open. We played outside all the time, discovering grapevines and paths that led us through nature. The smell of grass and corn growing mingled in the wind as we passed by, barefoot in the soft grass. It was the taste of freedom that all children love and need to grow up in a healthy way. My brother, Jason, and I had many of those carefree days growing up until one day it ended when our father, Pete, died. Suddenly, we grew up fast. It left a mark and a memory for me, and it became a way of healing as I cared for the children at Lar Feliz at the farmland that we had in Jaguariúna, Brazil.

I was at a training session on childcare with a few of the other workers. The material was the newest methods used in helping with child development. It was a pleasant surprise that there was a strong emphasis on child's play. In Brazil, we learned the importance of connecting to our inner child. Simply put, there was a happy memory inside each of us when we were children. That activity was more often something that we would be able to pass on to the children at the home. I had happy memories of seeing animals at my grandparents' farm, and I was able to pass that on to the children with whom I worked. The simplicity of play was a key that we used to help the little ones overcome their traumas and to grow.

"Play" involved many things in the leadership of the baby house. The idea was to keep their hands busy while talking and spending time together. At the baby house, it was done on a regular basis—at least a few times a week. Paintings were created and hung for all to see. Christmas cards were made in season and sold or given to friends. Fond memories of pleasant times were etched on our hearts and minds. At those moments around the table, it was clear to me that so many of the children were intelligent and had artistic talent. Some of them wanted to learn English, and they did so quickly and perfectly.

"Play" was baking imaginary cakes. It was blowing bubbles and even laughing and jumping in the rain. "Play" was going for long walks, visiting animals at the neighboring farms, and feeding the chickens. It was counting the butterflies at a nearby spring, and it was throwing little pebbles into a lake.

One day, when two little boys could not stop bickering, a picnic was prepared and brought on a hike into the woods behind the eating hall. There, a well-worn path led the workers and children to some beautiful sights. The fighting among the children abruptly ended; and they allowed themselves to be led gently by the hand to see the giant trees, plants, and breathtakingly beautiful gardens filled with God's creatures.

Learning to play musical instruments is something that we always encouraged at Lar Feliz. The music room, filled with fun, contained many percussion instruments and guitars, causing every wide-eyed child who entered to create music as a pastime. All these spontaneous moments were included in what we called "play," which helped to make a creative, intelligent, well-rounded, and happy child.

At the baby house, the most coveted items of the children were swings. At one point, there were swings hung from one end of the veranda to the other. The little ones would happily swing all afternoon, so long as the workers had the strength to push them.

One day, Claire, a volunteer from Ireland, brought a kite-making kit complete with some complicated instructions, colorful paper, skewer sticks made from bamboo, and some string and tape. A group of boys watched as she tried her best to explain in broken Portuguese. One boy, with his head leaned to the side, picked up some paper and some sticks and started folding the paper into a triangle and then a square. Another boy disappeared into the kitchen and returned with a small pair of scissors and a black garbage bag, which he proceeded to roll up and cut into long, thin strings. Another of the boys came from his room with an empty coffee can wrapped around with meters of string and a small stick tied to the end.

Claire came to teach them something that they had already known. One of the favorite pastimes in Brazil is the making and flying of kites. When driving along the slums on a breezy, sunny day, you can see various colorful kites flying high with a long tail made of cut up trash bags hanging below. As the children's heads are turned upward, gazing into the sky, they see a bright future sailing in the wind. They see an escape from the hopeless past, and they believe in joy again. As the kite flies like the wings of a butterfly, they are transformed into believing in a rebirth of a brighter tomorrow. They all know how to make their own kites, and they also know how to fly them.

Dinho was a professional musician who worked at Lar Feliz as a music teacher, and he also taught the learned value of children playing music. Oftentimes, when I came to work, worship music filled the farm. He formed bands with a guitar player, a drummer, a keyboard player, and a singer. There were many skilled musicians at Lar Feliz among the children; and they recorded some music, which turned out to be a blast.

He also loved to go to the baby house and perform a simple show for the little ones with his suitcase full of puppets. He had them sit down in the front while he held the puppets looking out through a small window. He did all the voices himself, and it was hilarious. The children were spellbound: watching, laughing, and even singing along in the middle of the afternoon. When everyone was hot and tired, Dinho came; and it was pure diversion and fun. Every time the children saw him heading over the hill to their house, they screamed with delight, jumping and clapping until he would open that suitcase filled with puppets, little percussion instruments, and all the fun that went together with music and children.

CHAPTER 22

# Walking in the Haunted Wood

*"Fear thou not; for I am with thee: be not dismayed; for I am thy God: I will strengthen thee; yea, I will help thee; yea, I will uphold thee with the right hand of my righteousness."*

Isaiah 41:10

In order to travel from Holambra to Lar Feliz, we had to take a dirt road through the woods. During the rainy season, it became very hard to pass through. A big truck with four-wheel drive could easily go through, but the average car would either slip and slide or get stuck. It was almost like driving through ice and snow in Ohio. When I drove this road in the middle of the day with my music playing and the breeze coming through the windows, I would often see a very large bright blue butterfly, the Blue Morphos, fly across the street to the woods.

On one side of the road into the grassy woods, there was a tiny, primitive house without a window or door, but a wall in the front was missing so that a person could see inside. The little house had no furniture in it at all—only a handful of little statues, some odd pieces of porcelain, and some bouquets of flowers that had been placed on the ground in and around the opening.

Small, foot-high statues of Mary and a few more of the saints that many churches would consider idols were placed on the ground. Later, I heard from someone in town that the house was a sort of temple where people came to do witchcraft or idol worship.

"You know that the people who live in Holambra believe that street is haunted!" said the hairdresser as she cut my hair one day. She knew a lot about the history and news of the town.

"You don't say!" I said with a look of surprise.

Later in the week, when I drove home from work, I saw some people walking. *Were they real or just ghosts?* I laughed out loud, and it was almost ridiculous to ask such a question.

Later that year, some volunteers arrived at the same time from two very different locations: Travis from Canada and a family from the Netherlands. Travis and Andrew had noticed the little house and were wondering what it was used for. One day, they even walked by it and noticed a strong rotten smell. There had been a dead animal laid there to rest, or could it have been an animal sacrifice? I could only wonder what had happened at that place in the woods.

They talked among themselves until they brought it to Paul's attention. Was there anything that could be done about the house? They thought that maybe it was their duty as Christians to destroy it.

"No, it is on private property, and you could get into a lot of trouble!" Paul said.

"You don't want any of those voodoo people to come after you once they realize that you destroyed their temple!" I said with a shiver running down my spine thinking about it.

"Those woods are not safe at night. There have been some thieves and bandits who have been hiding out there," Paul said.

It was true that although they were private property, the woods held no fences at the time; so, it was the perfect hiding place for drug deals or robbers. After the deed was done, they could hide; and no one would ever find them.

"Ridiculous," said Travis. "I'm not afraid of some little house on a dirt road!"

Many times, in the evenings at Lar Feliz, there were activities throughout the week like Bible studies and singing at a worship service. Travis had all kinds of fun ideas that usually took place after dinner before bedtime. Travis didn't own a car, but he rode his bike back and forth from the project to town where he rented a house. He chose to ride his bike through the haunted woods because it saved him a lot of time.

Travis heard all the advice; but he wasn't afraid, so he threw all the caution into the wind and used the dirt road that led through those woods. *"For God hath not given us the spirit of fear: but of power, and of love, and of a sound mind."*[12] He remembered the Word, and he wasn't buying into all those scary stories about things happening in the haunted wood.

For the first few weeks, he peddled through the deathly still, dark woods. There were no lamps at the side of the road to guide him, only his thin bike light that guided him through the thick darkness. He had to admit, it was very dark.

He continued riding home that way after dark until one night, something happened that scared him half to death. He recounted to us how all at once there were two big, bright headlights from a vehicle that were coming closer as he rode. They were headed his way! They didn't stop, but they just kept on moving closer and closer in his direction.

Even though he assured himself that he didn't believe in ghosts, he was still terrified as the lights came closer until they were only a meter away from his face before the vehicle screeched to a stop.

Then he told of the laughter that he heard.

"Ah ha ha ha! Ha ha ha! We got you Travis!" The Dutch man and his son were in the car laughing at Travis.

Travis, who was an ordained youth pastor and normally nonviolent, took one look at his friend and punched him in the face before he walked to the side of the road, got back on his bike, and peddled home.

---

[12] 2 Timothy 1:7

The Dutch man, who was about twice the size of Travis, sat for a minute, dumbfounded.

The Dutch volunteer still saw the humor in the situation even though he went home with a red mark on his face. The next morning when Travis came to apologize, he humbled himself; they shook hands, and we all had to laugh a little bit imagining how Travis hit the tall Dutch volunteer.

I often took that dirt road during the day through the beautiful jungle. It may have been a bumpy road; but it was still useful, and there was no reason to be afraid.

In 2019, on the dirt road that joined Holambra and Jaguariúna, two men shook hands in agreement. They were representatives of the two towns. The dirt road that passed through the haunted wood was a part of two towns. After many years of discussion, it was a possibility that the dirt road, a well-used road that led to a major highway, would finally be paved with asphalt.

The day came that all the workers and neighbors of Lar Feliz had been waiting for. There would be a better road to use to go back and forth to work. It had all come together because of a new condominium that was being constructed. The owners of the new expensive homes would have to use that dirt road to get home, and it would mean messing up their cars. Finally, progress!

CHAPTER 23

# A Song Sung in the Wilderness

*"Knowing this, that the trying of your faith worketh patience."*

James 1:3

## Amsterdam
1995

Terry Williams was an evangelist in Amsterdam who worked with Paul and me under STEM—Short Term Evangelistic Ministries. As the three of us prepared for an evangelistic outreach partnering with a church in a nearby city, Terry sang out loud with joy. Nothing could dampen his mood.

As we got into the car to leave, we noticed the sound equipment didn't turn on right away.

"That's okay, me duck!" he said as he went to the store around the corner to get some more batteries. At that point, the tape which held the music started to unwind.

"Well, I just happened to have another copy of that music," he said as he went to his desk for the cassette.

Finally, we got in the car to leave, and it started thundering with spring rain coming down. The car stuttered and wouldn't start.

"Terry, are you sure that we are supposed to do this outreach?" I asked. I was ready to give up and go home.

"Keep praying!" Terry said as the car finally started. "This outreach is going to be a blessing!" he shouted in between the verses of the song that he was singing.

As we drove along, the sun came out, drying up all the rain. We made it to the square on time where some Dutch, who were eager to get started, greeted us. Paul and Terry set up the evangelism area; and at last, Terry took the mic.

Terry pranced back and forth like a tiger, portraying how his life used to be and how it was now with Jesus.

"Jesus! Is there anyone here who wants to know Jesus? Now, I know that the minute I call upon the name of Jesus, many of you would like to walk away."

Some of the crowd bowed their heads and walked away, but there were some people who were intent on hearing what Terry had to say.

"I encourage the rest of you to stay! Did you know that a piercing changed my life?" Terry went on to talk about how Jesus had made him a new man and how the old was passed away because Terry had been a real scoundrel in his younger years.

"I used to be violent," Terry shared. Now, he rarely made it through a corny movie without the shedding of a few tears. "Jesus can change your life! Who of you would like to receive Him as Lord today?"

In the crowd, there were several hands going up. Groups were formed to pray for those who wanted to have a new life in Jesus.

It ended up being a blessed evening, one of those that I will always remember. Imagine if we had just given up and stayed home! What a lost opportunity that would have been; not only for us but also for the people who became followers of Jesus that day. It would have been a discouragement for that local church, who had been waiting. Terry was an old, experienced warrior; and he knew what would be ahead if he just kept trying.

Ronaldo began to play his guitar to the group of little boys who were sitting and standing along the large concrete table. He was the music teacher at Lar Feliz, and he also worked as a monitor. He was great with children, and he could teach music, too. Henrique, our Brazilian son, learned excellent guitar-playing skills from Ronaldo. I got out my flute to play along. I was relearning to play, working on the tone quality and playing by ear, which meant playing without sheet music. Ronaldo was originally from Rio. He was very patient, and he encouraged me to play along. He had a wonderful style and voice to listen to.

Ronaldo struck up a chorus about rain.

As we played the song and began to worship together, some men we didn't know arrived in white aprons with plastic head coverings and gloves. We continued to sing and didn't stop, even though the men were looking all around Lar Feliz, under tables and in the corners.

It was then that we realized we were being investigated by the health and sanitary police! They were making a surprise inspection. If Lar Feliz didn't pass, it would have to shut down. They investigated the bedrooms and the beds before making their way to the main kitchen. All the while, Paul was leading the way, answering questions and pointing out every corner of Lar Feliz. It was not unusual that Paul would be insulted and disrespected by the government officials, but he chose not to react at all. He was always polite and answered any question that arose about the children, the workers, or the home.

Ronaldo and I continued to play music with the children in a spirit of worship, even though it was unsettling to have this surprise visit. Lar Feliz passed the inspection, but there were a few recommendations that we were already in the process of addressing.

Sometimes, it was so tempting to just quit whenever a storm arose, but God had said in His Word to stand—just to stand. It was usually after that terrible storm passed that a big blessing came: people were saved; children were provided for; or a prayer was answered. All we had to do was keep standing and trusting God that everything would be all right; and in the end, it was.

One day, Ronaldo was singing a folk song in Portuguese to the small children who were jumping with smiling faces. I leaned in closer to hear it better. It was about a canoe that had tipped over. With each verse, a little child's name was inserted into the song, and the rest would sing along to the beautiful melody about the sea.

It was an old famous song in Brazil that I heard again while playing music for the children in the baby house. The melody was beautiful, something that you would long to sing along with while tapping your foot. In truth, the children at Lar Feliz seemed to have had a canoe tip over with the trauma they suffered in their broken homes. We all needed to be little fish and good swimmers to get to the bottom of that ocean, to rescue each child who was drowning below in the sea of their trial. To rescue the child from the bottom of the sea, one needed patience, perseverance, creativity, and faith.

Dinho, who was a talented musician, formed a small band from the children of the project. The band was invited to play at different venues; and everywhere they went, they spread joy. I was even invited to join the band and play my flute. One time, we played at a chicken-packing factory during the night shift. The chicken factories in Brazil were notorious for having a bad smell that drifted throughout the town. It was a good-paying job, but it wasn't the nicest place to work. The band practiced a lot; and we played the famous Brazilian folksongs, which were not easy to do, as well as well-known hymns.

Finally, the performance night came. As we were set up to play, in filed all kinds of men and women in white uniforms that covered their neck and head. They kept their gloves and masks on.

"You didn't tell me that we would be playing in the land of the Teletubbies!" I whispered to Dinho.

He laid his head back and roared with laughter. He kept laughing so hard that he could hardly get through his welcome speech. Afterward, on the way home, he kept saying, "Teletubbies!" He guffawed through the night. He would talk a little; then he would shake his head and start laughing all over again.

The men and women who worked at the chicken packing factory were so grateful that the music group had come from the children's home to sing their favorite songs. In a smelly factory where everyone was dressed alike, it was a "festa" with chords of lovely music winding its way throughout the halls.

## CHAPTER 24
# The Long Wait

*"But thou, O Lord, art a God full of compassion, and gracious, longsuffering, and plenteous in mercy and truth."*

Psalm 86:15

It was a long and winding road to home.

The teenage girl tossed her hair and gave a smile. "We will only be here for six months!" she said to me, referring to her little brother and sister.

They were a new family that had been received by Lar Feliz. They had a mom and a dad who loved them, but the mom was addicted to drugs. She only had to finish her time at a recuperation shelter to bring her children home. It seemed as if it would be an easy ending to a difficult time, but it turned out to be anything but easy.

The older sister was very loyal to her parents. She forgave them, and she believed everything that they had told her. The desire was strong for the parents to bring their children home. Six months passed by; and finally, the family of five could enjoy visits together in the living room of Lar Feliz, where two of the smaller children were staying.

It had been hard to leave their children in a shelter. They were from a strict church, and they didn't like everything they saw. They had a narrow vision of the right way that things should be done, and the Lar Feliz monitors didn't fit into their way of caring. They developed a negative attitude toward the workers and the technical team. The unhappy couple found ways to frustrate the workers and staff with their complaints and lies. They even stole new shoes from the clothes cupboards they hoped to sell in town for a profit. They showed up unannounced and without our permission to school events and activities of the children who then became more and more distressed. The youngest of the three would cry at the smallest of occasions.

As the grumbling parents became more unhappy and discontented with their situation, the children also became very sad; and a crisis was about to erupt that would leave the family changed—never to be the same again.

When the grumbling parents had run out of critical things to say about the Lar Feliz staff, they began to criticize one another. They fought and began to point out one another's faults. The father blamed and punished the mother, and she did likewise to him until they finally decided to separate. The mother, who was alone without anyone to help, fell back into drugs. She would now need to do another stint in a rehabilitation home. As a result, they would forever lose the opportunity to parent their own children.

During the time that it had taken the grumbling parents to sort out their own personal rubbish, their family of three children had continued to grow. The oldest of the siblings was now an adolescent. The three children had their own needs that couldn't wait or be set aside while the parents did their fixing. They would need to be placed for adoption in order for them to have the best possible lives. They would have their own belongings and beds. They would have their own home, where they would grow up and one day come back to visit. They would have grand birthday parties with their new parents who would teach them many things. They would laugh and giggle together. They would find true love, and they would be reborn in a couple's heart. They would finally be adopted.

When the day came for the adoptive couple to meet the three siblings, the warm smile and hugs of the attractive woman melted the children's hearts and easily broke down any barriers. The youngest of the siblings crawled into the lap of their new father. They gathered what belongings they had from Lar Feliz, and they happily and willingly traveled miles and miles to reach their new forever home.

CHAPTER 25
# Inside Out

*"Things are not always as they seem."*[13]

—Phaedrus

A picnic was planned for a holiday; and the children from the baby house were loaded up with blankets, a barbecue kit, some nice cuts of meat, some limes, and salads. A package of seasonings was also put into the picnic bag with everything needed for a wonderful outing. The whole baby house went along with a family of three brothers. They were all well-behaved because they were having the time of their lives, and it became a wonderful picnic and day. All the children ate rice, along with the meat, beans, and potato salad. They drank lime juice practically the whole day. Everything went smoothly; and they came home to rest, shower, and go to bed.

The next morning, the other shift of monitors arrived; and as they dressed the children, one of the monitors looked at the legs and arms of one of the little boys who had been to the picnic.

"What happened here?" she asked as she held her hand to her mouth looking at the little boy's arms and legs. What could have gone wrong with such a wonderful picnic?

---

13  Phaedrus, *The Fables of Phaedrus*, trans. P.F. Widdows (Austin: University of Texas Press, February 1, 1992).

The parents arrived soon to visit their three boys.

"What happened here?" the father asked. With his hand, he motioned toward the little boy's arms and legs. The color had deepened into what appeared to be a very bad bruising.

"I really don't know what happened, but it doesn't seem to bother him any," said the day monitor. She took one finger and ran it along the bruised leg to see if the child had reacted at all. Nothing had been mentioned in the communication book. The little boy was just as happy as ever, and he continued to eat everything set on the table. There was soda, cheesy chips, and cookies. He smiled and smacked his lips, licking his fingers as he ate.

The technical team had been notified, and the monitor who had planned the picnic was brought to the office to be questioned.

"I promise, there was no fighting or rough playing at the picnic. Everyone sat and ate and had a grand time."

"Was there any lotion or sunscreen put on the children?" asked the social worker on staff as an idea began to materialize in her mind of what could have happened.

"Maybe only a little lime juice that I had on my hands," she replied.

They thought that perhaps the little boy had a reaction to the lime juice that touched his skin, and he was brought to the doctor for some tests.

After an agonizing battery of tests, the doctor had a diagnosis. What looked like a case of abuse or beating turned out to be an allergy to food coloring! What made matters worse was that in Brazil, the food coloring agent was put in many foods and seasonings. It is found in most soft drinks, in ketchup and mustard, and even in chocolate!

It was Easter time. Groups came and went, and they brought with them chocolate eggs. Each child at Lar Feliz accumulated at least three large chocolate eggs before Easter season ended.

The little boy was found pouting by himself as the others ate their chocolate; but the monitors brooded over him like eagles, not letting any food with a hint of coloring pass his lips. While the other children could have their strawberry yogurt, he could only have a glass of milk. When chicken stroganoff was being served with a hint of ketchup, he would have to eat only plain meat and rice. Even his family who came to visit had to be careful of what snacks they could bring.

Then one day, all the purple patches on his skin had completely disappeared, and he was better. He was also a little thinner, and his tummy had gone flat. He was the healthiest that he had ever been. What appeared to be bruising on the outside was a reaction to what was happening on the inside of the little boy's body—an allergy to food coloring.

Only a few short weeks later, the three sons were returned home to their parents, who had gotten rid of anything that would hinder them from taking good care of their family. The home was checked to find that it was ready for the three boys to return, and they did. The parents were so happy, and the three children were also equally happy!

CHAPTER 26

# Home Is Not a Place

*"Home is not where you are from, it is where you belong. Some of us travel the whole world to find it. Others, find it in a person."*[14]

—Beau Taplin

## Guarulhos Airport
2015

"I'm sorry there is absolutely no way that you will make your connection on time. Would you like to change your tickets for $600 each?"

Unable to reach Paul by phone, I looked at Jeremy, who was traveling with me to Ohio.

"Six hundred dollars is a lot of money, son. What do you think we should do?"

Jeremy nodded as if reading my mind; and I answered the clerk at the desk, "Well, ma'am, we are sure going to try!"

My hands shook as I checked in. Paul had accidentally booked our tickets wrong, having us land in New York, with our connecting flight to Cleveland, Ohio, leaving from Newark airport. We had exactly one hour for Jeremy and me to get our luggage, go through customs, and take a shuttle to Newark to

---

14  Beau Taplin, *Buried Light* (Beau Taplin, 2016).

board our flight that would take us to Ohio. It seemed impossible, but we were going to try.

Isa had already moved to Ohio to start her adult life. She started out working at a café, and she took some courses from a community college. My heart, which lived in two different places, was happy for her that she was doing so well. She continued to prosper and do well at everything that she set her hand to do; her only work experience in Brazil was working by my side in the baby house at Lar Feliz, taking care of the toddlers.

Through her work at Lar Feliz, she came to a deeper understanding of why we had moved to Brazil in the first place. She saw a little boy transform from an angry, fist-clenched rascal to a child as sweet as pudding who made her cry when she said goodbye. As Jeremy and I traveled to see her, it made me realize that in just a few years, Jeremy would be moving there, too.

As the plane took off, we stretched out and chose movies to watch, not thinking about when we would land. I had come to enjoy long flights overseas to read a book and have some quiet time that I craved in our busy house back in Brazil. Paul was not going on this trip, but he was staying at home with our teenage Brazilian son, Henrique, to hold down the fort.

"I'm sorry, can we cut through? We have a connecting flight to catch," I said to the family planted directly in front of me. *"Da licensa,"* I said in Portuguese.

To our surprise, the line seemed to open down the middle like the parting of the Red Sea, and we walked through. Once off the plane, we began to jog our way to customs. As most of the visitors that morning were Brazilians and not American citizens, we had little time to wait in line. Grabbing our suitcases, we quickly made our way to the exit in record time and tried to find our shuttle bus to Newark.

"Girl, you better go! Your plane is leaving in only forty minutes!" said the attendant who checked our tickets. "You get one of those cabs and go!"

Jeremy and I didn't hesitate as we popped into the nearest cab. The driver was friendly, and he had a certain accent.

"Yes, ma'am, I'll get you there! Don't worry about a thing!" he assured us.

I was not accustomed at all to New York City and was a little bit nervous. As Jeremy and I looked out the windows at the city that was just waking up, we could finally relax. Maybe we would make it after all. The skilled taxi driver glided from one lane to the next, pointing out landmarks to us as he went.

"This here is the Brooklyn Bridge. We are almost there now."

I fumbled with my bank card and later learned I accidentally paid him twice. It was worth it. The brakes squealed to a stop right in front of the check-in desk.

"Jeremy van Opstal? Jill van Opstal? Are you traveling to Cleveland, Ohio, today?"

"Yes!" Jeremy said as he maneuvered our two big suitcases by himself.

"Congratulations! You just made your flight. The attendant was about to close the door."

"Thank you, Lord," I said. We had achieved what was impossible.

After we arrived in Ohio, my brothers asked how the flight was.

"It's a long story!" I replied.

"We are just glad that you made it home," my mom said.

In just a few short years, Jeremy would have another layover in New York on his way from Amsterdam to Ohio. I worried and didn't feel ready to let him go, but he was fine. He was on a new adventure; and he would begin his life in the USA, where he would receive blessing upon blessing while working hard at whatever job he could find.

It was hard for Paul and me to see our kids move so far away. When we were young, we also moved far away from our families; but we always returned home to visit, as they would. I knew that God still had a calling on my life to do more in Brazil, and new doors opened for me to serve as well as to learn and to grow.

"Home" as a place is a myth, and I learned that I could feel at home just about anywhere. Jesus makes His home inside us; and wherever we are, we are no longer alone.

## CHAPTER 27
## *Under Protest*

*"Behold, how good and how pleasant it is
for brethren to dwell together in unity!"*

Psalm 133:1

Lar Feliz was made up of children from different cities who were brought there by order of the judge. The children came from high-risk situations, where the children faced danger on a regular basis. Gradually, through the years, Paul and the technical staff began to see this change regarding the teenagers who came to Lar Feliz. Lately, the teens came not only from nice homes and families, but they were also a threat to their own families! This was a completely different situation because the little ones who were so broken were generally happy when they came to live at Lar Feliz. They enjoyed it so much that they didn't really want to leave at first. Many of the little ones were placed for adoption with new families and homes.

Contrarily, the teens were brought to Lar Feliz under protest. They didn't want to be there. Many of them had used drugs in the past, and they had committed small crimes as well. Some of the girls were prostitutes on the streets to earn money.

Sometimes, they were also drug-users. At Lar Feliz, we received teenage mothers with their babies, and both had to be cared for. It also became common that a baby was brought whose mother had used drugs while she was pregnant. We saw babies suffer the bad effects of withdrawal. As the world grew harsher, it was hard to see. The workers were sometimes tired. Sometimes, they gave up on a particular teenager. The teenagers knew how to push the buttons of the workers. For that reason, it was generally recommended not to share very much about one's background, issues, past, or family problems. It had happened more than once that a worker left in tears, unable to cope with the teenagers.

"You can't say that about my child!" Monica said through her sobs. She furiously washed the rest of the dishes before putting her belongings in her purse. She had had enough. It was over now.

"After all that I have done for you, how can you say such things?" she raised her voice again to the troublesome teen mother.

She wasn't the only one who left in tears. There were other workers who couldn't work one more day after trying to reach the teenage girls. Monica had been the activities director who would plan arts and crafts and trips for the children. She had done amazing work. Somehow, one of the teenage girls had found out about Monica's son, who had suffered with health problems and eventually died.

It was often a fact that the teenage girls were more difficult to work with than the boys. One teenage girl could form a whole pack that would gang up on the workers and create misery. The workers had to find the balance of being a friend or being an authority figure. This was an art to do perfectly, and many had failed. A very good worker would work for a time; and then something would take place, causing a burnout and a desire to never return to work again. If a worker did fun things with the teenage girls and was always their friend, it would eventually backfire. Bringing any child to one's own home for the holidays or weekends also proved to be a mistake. It created too strong of a bond between the worker and the child; and sadly, one day, the child would take advantage of it.

Even though working with teenagers was not always easy, there were many instances where it turned out to be good. Usually, after they became eighteen and went to live on their own, they would keep in contact. Sometimes, they would write or visit; and sometimes, they would apologize for what they did wrong. Most of the time, they were appreciative of what they had experienced at Lar Feliz.

The dining hall had tables and chairs lined up with espresso, coconut cake, and colored napkins. There were clotheslines hung on opposite walls where various pictures were hanging. There were pictures of babies and toddlers, family groupings with siblings, arm in arm. Most of them were smiling, except for a few funny faces made. They were pictures of happy times and splendid memories.

"If you see yourself in one of these pictures, please feel free to take them home," I said with a loud voice above the rumble of voices that had filled the dining hall. Over two hundred adults had gathered for a Lar Feliz reunion. Some came to reminisce; others were curious; but most came to say thanks to Pastor Paul, myself, the technical team, the monitors, and the cooks.

"Thank you for giving me such a good start in life!" said Thiago. "I was able to buy my own home."

Chris, with a beautiful baby on his hip, came up and shook Paul's hand.

"How are you?" Paul asked quietly, emotion in his words. "What was your name again? Ah yes, I remember you now!"

I tilted my head to the side as a tall, handsome young couple came up to me with outstretched hands. All the kids had grown up; and as adults, it was hard to place their faces with their names and the memories of the sweet young lives they had. Over two thousand children had been helped by Lar Feliz since it had opened ten years earlier. It was a milestone, a victory. It hadn't always been easy, but we had made it through!

"I'm Caique," said a dark-haired man.

"Oh, yes!" A picture of a young Caique came to mind: a clever, squirrelly blond boy with vibrant green eyes.

Some of the kids who had grown up at Lar Feliz went through rough times after they left. Some got into drugs; some went to prison; and a few even died. Even though most of them lived fruitful and productive lives, it was still painful to hear of the ones who didn't. Even a prison cell couldn't quench out a life completely. A few of the boys had done time and came out completely new. I saw one such boy at a grocery store in a town nearby.

"Hey, Tía Jill!"

I spun around in the fruit and vegetable department at a large grocery in Athur, Nogueira.

"Do you remember me?" asked a handsome, well-groomed young man in a work apron.

"I remember your face and your smile, but I can't quite remember your name. Where are you from?"

"My two brothers and I spent some months at Lar Feliz."

"Oh, yes, I remember you now! How have you been? It's so good to see you!"

"I'm doing better now, Tía Jill. I really loved the time with Lar Feliz; but when we were sent home, we had such hard times." He spilled out memories of fighting parents, substance abuse, and moving from home to home. "I'm better now," he reassured me.

Paul and I knew that we could help as many children as we were able, but it wasn't possible to help every single one. Some would not receive help; some weren't ready to be helped. It was a harsh reality.

We learned from a Baptist pastor in Ohio, "You won't be able to help them all! That you must remember! Kids will come and go. Some will do well, but others won't. It is something that you must live by, or else you will get discouraged. I know. I have been there. I was a foster parent for years," he stated.

Some advice was just as valuable as funds. Instead of being discouraged to start our mission, we were enlightened and better prepared. There was something extra special about gleaning a shiny pearl of wisdom from someone who had experience.

William gently held the white rabbit in his hands. He cared for it daily, bringing it water and food. He named it Bella. William—a fifteen-year-old boy, who was tall and thin with a long ponytail down his back—was a gentle spirit who loved animals, peace, and plants. He got along with most of the boys in the house, and he was always fondly remembered by the staff and children.

One day, it was time for him to go back home to his family. The situation there had improved, and he would work a part-time job to help with the costs of the home. Bella would go with him; he was her sole caretaker, and he also brought a few meager belongings.

It would be a new start and a new day. He would finish school in the evenings, and he would work at the grocery store during the day. Everyone from the technical team felt pretty good about him going home, and it was one of the greatest success stories. He would live with his father, even though they had not had any contact for years.

Years later, the staff received bad news about William; he had been shot and killed. There was not a lot of information given out by the family.

"Was it drug-related?" the staff asked each other.

It turned out that he had been in the wrong place at the wrong time. There were a lot of the details of the story that had been missing like how a gentle, God-loving, hardworking young man had been gunned down by violence.

Drug addiction in Brazil was at the highest of proportions, touching almost everyone. It seemed to be the biggest problem and threat to society. Corruption in Brazil is the number one threat to democracy, but drugs had to be the number one threat to the family. Many were wounded in its destructive wake. Drugs affected every sector of society.

After a few days, we heard from one of the workers named Marcelo that William had been in a church service where a strong message was preached right before he died.

"The Lord is calling you to come to Him, and He is knocking on the door!" the fiery preacher had said. "Come to this altar and get right with the Lord!"

Marcelo recalled how William sat and appeared to listen; but instead of answering the altar call, he quietly stood to his feet and began to exit out the back but not before catching the attention of the preacher ending his invitation!

"Young man! Do not leave this church! God has a plan for you! Do not leave, or your life will be cut short!" he emphasized as a last pitch to get William to the altar.

William did not heed the preacher's pleading; but instead, he headed out into the night and was later gunned down. The circumstances were unclear.

He left behind him many who loved him. Many grieved, and he would be missed; but his life had a purpose after all. His story would change the lives of others.

## CHAPTER 28
# Don't Cry, Baby, Don't Cry!

*"Blessed be God, even the Father of our Lord Jesus Christ, the Father of mercies, and the God of all comfort; Who comforteth us in all our tribulation, that we may be able to comfort them which are in any trouble, by the comfort wherewith we ourselves are comforted of God."*

2 Corinthians 1:3-4

"Don't cry, baby, don't cry," I said to the twin named Renee as I held her hand and walked where a group of visitors were standing with shovels.

A group of teachers and students from a private school Isa was attending came to visit Lar Feliz. Brazil had a holiday for just about every occasion, and this one was dedicated to the planting of trees. They had brought with them various trees to plant at the farm. Spread out in a valley with many different types of trees, the students and the teachers planned to plant in a forsaken little patch of dry land.

*Hopefully, they will grow*, I thought to myself.

"Come, children, let's help them plant some trees!" I said as I took their hands and led them to the little valley below. It turned out to be a wonderful day for students, teachers, and children alike. The school learned that Lar Feliz was a happy place to be with children laughing and playing. The twins,

Renee and Randy, caught everyone's attention. They were so cute but also full of mischief.

Around a week later, I received the most horrible news. I received a call around midnight from my mom that my brother Rick had suddenly passed away. It turned out to be a very tragic time for the whole family, and I decided to fly home to Ohio to be a help wherever needed.

"It's up to you," my mom said. "We, as a family, can help pay for your ticket if you want to come."

I needed to go home to the family in Ohio, where we could grieve together and hold one another up during this most difficult time. We would remember all the happy times of years past. We would crack jokes like Rick used to do; we would remember all the funny things that he had said; and we would have a pocket full of happiness during the dark moment where Jesus is the only Light.

While wiping away the tears, Paul and I organized my flight home to Ohio; but first, I would go to work for one morning at Lar Feliz to the baby house and explain that I must go away for a little while.

Once I arrived, my heart raw with pain, I was surprised to have the children run up to me, giving hugs and crying.

"We are so sorry to hear about your brother, Rick, passing away. We are so sorry, Tía Jill!" They formed a group hug and began to cry softly together.

Renee's eyes searched my face, and she asked earnestly, "Tía Jill, is that your only brother who died, or do you have any more brothers?"

"Why, I have four more brothers who are alive!"

Relief washed over Renee's little face as she said, "Oh, I am so happy that you have some more brothers, Tía Jill!"

At that, I laughed; and we all shared a chuckle together.

I flew home, where I was surrounded by family grieving the loss together: hugging, crying, laughing, and eating chicken dinners in memory of Rick. His loss would be felt by all he left behind but especially by his wife, Lisa, and his children, Jacob and Rachel. Rick was a machinist and a carpenter, and he could make about anything beautiful out of wood. He built a log cabin in the woods, where they lived. Now, he was resting in the strong arms of the perfect Carpenter in Heaven, Jesus, the Son of God.

About six months later, my mom decided to visit Brazil. She loved the weather with its beautiful mornings and sunshine every day. She loved the shops and going out to eat. She also loved to see the baby house that I oversaw.

We went for a walk along the road to visit the animals at the farm nearby. Since Judy, my mom, was a twin herself, she liked being with the twins, Renee and Randy; and she took them each by the hand as they walked along.

Suddenly, Renee knew she had to tell Mom something. Mom, who was only able to understand English, bent down to hear what Renee was trying to say. Renee placed her small brown hands on each side of Mom's face and said the only words in English she knew.

"I love you!" she said brightly. And when she noticed that Mom understood, she said it again and again.

The toddlers had all learned to say "Judy," and they would say it at all different times like a hot pan of popcorn popping on the stove. "Judy, Judy, Judy." When Renee said those magical words, "I love you," it pierced through the clouds, shining joy. Mom smiled and cried simultaneously.

Grief comes in waves. Suddenly, the feelings come without warning and just as quickly leave again. One must learn to float.

"Whatever string you can find to hold on to, whatever you know about God in your heart, hang on to it with everything that you have. Then stand back and see His glory!"[15]

Mom had a wonderful visit in Brazil, and she went back to her home in Ohio while I stayed in Brazil and poured myself into my work.

---

15　Bill Dunn and Kathy Leonard, *Through a Season of Grief* (Nashville: Thomas Nelson, 2021), 116.

In Brazil, there is a saying that goes something like this: "I will hide my own pain while I will help you with yours." It is a sign of true friendship—laying down your own feelings while helping someone else through their hard times.

Lar Feliz continued to grow and flourish while I continued to plant seeds. I cried in the shadows, but I held God's promise from Psalm 126:5-6 in my heart. *"They that sow in tears shall reap in joy. He that goeth forth and weepeth, bearing precious seed, shall doubtless come again with rejoicing, bringing his sheaves with him."*

Soon, it was time for Renee and Randy to be placed for adoption, together with the other two brothers and one sister.

"I can't be placed for adoption, Tía Jill. Do you know why?"

"Tell me why." I was stunned.

"My new mother has one eye that is bigger than the other."

"Really? You don't say!"

"Really, Tía Jill."

"Does she have two arms to hold you and give hugs?"

"Yes, she does."

"What about a mouth to give you a big smile?"

Renee nodded as she was deep in thought.

"Why don't you and I make some pictures to give her as a present?"

"Okay."

Every day, Renee made a new drawing; they were colorful expressions of who she was and the world around her. At the end of the week, when the prospective couple arrived, she handed them a bag full of artistic creations. The woman, who was a schoolteacher, adored them and complimented the toddler, while pointing out her natural talent. It was a successful adoption indeed.

"Pastor, Pastor, I had the strangest dream!" Chris shouted as Paul and I arrived at the project one morning.

Whenever we arrived at Lar Feliz—no matter the time of day—there were always swarms of teens and children—and sometimes workers—who had to talk with Paul. If he wasn't at Lar Feliz, then he had rivers of messages coming in on his phone tagged as "urgent."

Paul usually had over a hundred things on his mind, one of them being that the milk supply was getting low.

Trusting the Lord seemed to come easier for me while Paul was left to organize paying all the bills. He trusted the Lord, but he said that he would like to see things move along a little faster sometimes. He knew that the Lord's timing was perfect, but it was a lesson that he was still learning.

"God always provided for us; He will do it again, won't He?" I said to him as a reminder. In the past, the Lord had supplied everything that we needed in miraculous ways.

On this particular day, his eyes swept through the crowd to see Cristiano, the excitement beaming from his face.

"Okay, Cristiano, what was your dream?" Paul asked, a little impatiently. He had a few minutes before his meeting would start.

"I dreamed that a big bus came, no it was more like a truck," he started. "The big truck came with lots of milk for the project, and Santa Claus was on it. And my mother was on it, too, and she was coming to see us for the first time!"

Paul patted him on the head. "That is a very nice dream. Wouldn't that be so nice if all of that happened?" he asked as he passed by another teen, who also had a couple questions.

It was mid-December in Brazil. Christmas was on the way, and it was hot as blazes. It was typical for Brazilian families to have a barbecue on Christmas Eve followed by a midnight swim in the pool. In the afternoon, when the air felt like an oven, the workers and children stayed indoors with the shutters closed and cartoons playing on the TV with the cool cement floors beneath their feet.

At around 4:00 or 5:00 in the afternoon, a horn could be heard in the distance. The persistent honking gradually grew closer, until it seemed to be coming right in front of the farm, awakening some from a deep nap.

"What is it?" One of the workers stuck his head out of the office to see.

Children and adults came outside into the driveway in front of the farm to see where all the noise was coming from.

Cristiano came outside and began to shout, "Look, look, would you look!" Tears from his eyes made a path down his face to the bottom of his chin. "I told you it would happen," he said as he looked in Pastor Paul's direction.

There in front of them was a big semi pulling a trailer that was open in the back to reveal Santa Claus waving. He was arm in arm with an older woman, who turned out to be the mother of Cristiano who had not been able to visit her children for years.

Santa helped her to step down off the trailer; and some other adults also came out, greeting Paul and the children that were there. Their arms were filled with presents wrapped in crinkly red and white paper. As they reached the children and the staff, one of them exclaimed, "Oh, we almost forgot; we brought you a month's supply of milk!"

The look on Paul's face was priceless!

"Wasn't that just like God? God is in the miracle business!"

Paul told the story to as many as he could when he explained how God provided at Lar Feliz. He said that simple statement to couples who were without hope. He said it when explaining to supporters who saw a need. He proclaimed it at Sunday evening church. That simple statement was something that God taught him during the last hour of need on a hot summer afternoon. The truth of Philippians 4:19 became ingrained in a memory: *"But my God shall supply all your need according to his riches in glory by Christ Jesus."*

CHAPTER 29

# New Places

*"Wherefore glorify ye the LORD in the fires, even the name of the LORD God of Israel in the isles of the sea."*

Isaiah 24:15

"Where should we take our friend Regine for vacation in Brazil?" Paul asked me over a cup of coffee one morning.

With excitement, we called around and looked on the internet for a wonderful place to take our friend—a widow from the Netherlands who needed a vacation. Brazil was an endless land with many unusual things to see. We settled on a Swiss-style village called Campo do Jordan followed by a trip to a beautiful beach at Caraquatatuba. We hoped and prayed that every detail would be perfect for our beloved friend.

We took her by car to the village. The little Brazilian town had the feel of old Europe. The luxurious hot chocolate at the café warmed the soul in the cool open air. We walked along the streets and shops and enjoyed violin music from the master hand of a street musician. We enjoyed steak dinner with potatoes and broccoli; and after a long weekend, we came back to Holambra. It was cozy—or, in Dutch, we would say "gezellig!" Our friend, Regine, enjoyed the time.

When we returned, she met up with some Dutch friends in Holambra. Next, we planned a week at the beach, Caraquatatuba. We were all looking forward to this relaxing break. The trip was about five hours through the highways and the mountains. We looked off into the distance at the most gorgeous views until finally we arrived at the five-star hotel. When we got to our rooms, the plans of showing Regine a wonderful place began to unravel.

"No one helps with the luggage here?" Regine asked quietly as Paul struggled getting our suitcases situated in each room.

"My room is all the way in another wing. I was hoping that we would be situated close by, seeing as how I don't speak Portuguese!"

"Let's drop our bags off and worry about that later. I'm getting hungry! Let's go see what we can find in town!" Paul said while heading to the desk to make the changes.

The head clerk nodded his head with an artificial smile. Satisfied with his answer and having great energy, we decided to go for a walk around the town. We scoured the area looking for some nice shops and restaurants and some incredible views, but we came to a seedy neighborhood.

"Where are we?" I asked as if we had taken a wrong turn. There were no shops or restaurants—at least none were open. We continued to walk along in the hot afternoon sun.

"Maybe we can find a grocery store to buy us a few snacks until the restaurants open," said Paul.

"That's a good idea!" said Regine.

We came across a jam-packed grocery store. Everywhere we looked, there were beach-goers in bathing suits with dirty sandals on their feet. The aisles were packed with children and even the occasional mangy dog. Regine looked back and forth, and her eyes were noticing everything. The three of us walked along, buying drinks, buns and cheese, and some apples. We stood out among the crowd, like blue roses in a forest of trees. Subconsciously, we huddled together as we got into the long checkout line.

A group of young men buying sodas were laughing and jostling in front of us when suddenly, one of the cans slipped through his long fingers and exploded on the floor, showering Regine's white cashmere sweater with brown, fizzy bubbles.

"Oh!" Regine was startled and shouted in Dutch, "Hey, guy, watch what you are doing!"

"It was an accident," Paul said.

"Let's hurry up and get out of here!" I whispered as we finally reached the front of the line.

Paul hastily paid for the groceries, and we headed back to the five-star hotel. Regine was happy to get a new key to a room closer to ours. Taking a moment, I looked out the window and went on the veranda to breathe in the fresh ocean breeze.

"Paul, can you quickly take a picture?" Photography is a hobby, and I loved to capture every moment on film to remember.

"Okay!" Paul shouted from the bathroom. "I've got some bad news!" There had been a water leak in the bathroom, which left five inches of water on the floor. "I'll call the desk!"

As the maid service came with an arm load of towels to mop up the water, Regine said quietly, "You need to ask for a new room! Don't put up with this kind of stuff!"

Paul went to the desk, listening to the staff member's assurances that it would be fixed. We decided to go out for the evening and asked for directions to the nearest restaurant. A steak place near the beach was indicated. We went and enjoyed the meal until the check came. The exorbitant amount was enough to buy groceries for a modest Brazilian family for a month.

We went back to our rooms. The bathroom was still leaking. Paul got the key to a new room with a working bathroom, but it was minus the view.

"Well, you can't get everything you want," I said, determined to make the best of it. Tomorrow would be a great day.

The next morning, the sun was twinkling brightly as we drank our coffee in the hotel restaurant. Our table was generously laden with fruits and bread.

"I vote we go to the beach!"

"I second the vote!" Regine said.

We gathered our things and quickly walked down. Upon arriving by the stirring waters, Regine looked unimpressed, disappointment marking her forehead.

"Where are the chairs? Are we supposed to lay on the sand?"

"I saw some chairs for sale. I will go buy you one!" Paul said as he grabbed his wallet.

"I love to swim in the ocean. I will be back in an hour," I said.

I loved to ride the waves like a dolphin; the rocking saltwater had a way of easing my tension. Paul quickly returned with some lawn chairs. Regine put on her hat and took out a book to read. For lunch, we bought the catch of the day: fried, breadcrumb batter fish with some French fries. We squeezed lime juice on the top. It was good, as well as inexpensive. The day at the beach was over, and we came back to the desk to get the key.

"Was everything okay, sir?" the suave man at the desk asked Paul as we brought our dirty towels to the bin to be washed.

"Yes, we had a great time," Paul replied. "Any ideas of places nearby that we can visit?"

"You cannot leave without seeing Ilhabela. It is breathtaking!" the man at the desk said. He gave directions to Paul on how to get there. "It is just a quick trip on the ferry. You can spend the day and then come back at night."

"What do you think?" Paul asked.

"Yeah, that sounds nice."

We were both willing to go. After all, if it was just a quick trip, it would be worth it; and we were ready for an adventure!

We got on the highway and drove to the ferry. The long line consisted of semi-trucks and about one hundred bicycles driven by young boys. There were beat-up jalopies, vacation-goers, and people of all kinds waiting in line. We chatted and talked, and the time dragged on. The midday hot Brazilian sun came out, melting ice cream cones and reddening the skin. We started to get hungry as we waited until finally, it was time to pull on to the ferry boat with our car. The tension of the wait evaporated as we parked the car and walked to the front of the ferry to get a view of the ocean waves. The sea wind nearly blew off Regine's hat!

Once we arrived, we were in awe of the beauty surrounding us. The color of the sea matched the clear blue sky, which was a glittering shade of turquoise. Everywhere, the women were walking in their beach dresses and "Havaianas." The palm trees swayed with a welcoming hello. On the clean, rocky coast was a row of little restaurants to buy a cold drink or the catch of the day. We walked a little further until we saw the sign. It read "Pimenta de Cheiro" with a little red pepper on it, and it sat atop the brightly painted building by the sea.

"Why don't we go here?" Regine asked. We entered and sat at a rustic, wooden table near the sand of the beach. We looked at the lunch menu and saw that the special of the day was steak and fries! Every meal came with rice and beans and salad. After we enjoyed a wonderful meal together, Regine paid the bill. I swam a little bit in the clean waters of the beach, while Regine went for a long walk along the shore. Paul sat at a table nearby, sipping his drink. The day could not get any better!

As we got in our car to return to the hotel, the sun was setting, creating a beautiful purple-orange sky. This time, there was not a line to go on the ferry; and we glided right through. After a few more days, we would drive the five hours back to Holambra.

"We are not only friends, but we are also family," Regine said as she left to go to the airport.

After all the places that we had traveled to in Brazil, her favorite place was Holambra. She gave us a warm hug, and the next time we would see her would be in the Netherlands.

The trip with Regine was the first time Paul and I had seen Ilhabela, but it would not be the last.

## CHAPTER 30
## Brother to Brother

*"And the Lord said unto Cain, 'Where is Abel thy brother?'*
*And he said, 'I know not: Am I my brother's keeper?'"*

Genesis 4:9

Santo Antonio de Posse and Jaguariúna—two cities that brought children to Lar Feliz—were like two brothers who had outgrown each other after time. Santo Antonio de Posse (Posse) had been bringing their children to Lar Feliz almost from the very beginning. Over half of the inhabitants of the children were from Posse, and there were fewer from Jaguariúna. Of the children who came, many were from excruciating circumstances. The lives and faces of the children were unforgettable.

According to political officials, when the number of cases had exceeded twenty children, it was time for the town to start their own children's home. The number of children from Posse that had been sent to Lar Feliz had grown to twenty-eight!

All the children who came had found a warm place in each of our hearts at Lar Feliz. It would be devastating to see them all go back to Posse, where they were originally from. There were teenage girls and boys who had lived most of their lives at Lar Feliz, but was it a political thing?

Changes were happening everywhere in Brazil. New theories were being put into practice. At times, it felt insecure, like the rules had suddenly all been thrown away. Paul and I—and the other workers at Lar Feliz, who had years of experience—had some doubts about how it would work. With more than half of the children leaving at once, many of the workers would have to leave and find work somewhere else. There would be financial burdens after one town who had paid the stipulated amount of expenses would no longer need services.

What would happen to Lar Feliz? Was this the beginning of the end of a home that brought joy to so many children and families?

Around the table, some of the strongest supporters sat as Pastor Paul explained how things would be changing. In the past, the average number of children was forty. Now, we would downsize to under twenty! As Paul bravely explained on, my heart leaked out through my tears; and I brushed them away with a tissue.

When times of discouragement came on us like a cloud, little seeds of hope began to appear.

"Did you know that there is a need of a children's home at Ilhabela?" Paul asked the technical team.

"Where did you find that out?" one of the psychologists asked.

It was a different method that the state started using. It was called a "chamada publico," or a public calling. This new procedure was carried out by the public administration to organize activities or projects that were of public interest. Only those with registration in order showing that they have a competent work record may apply. They needed new management for their children's home located on the beautiful beach of Ilhabela! First, we would have to visit and spy out the land before we would put our bid in for Lar Feliz to take over. We would rent a van and go there together.

Pastor Paul rented a van big enough for twenty people; and bright and early, the main workers arrived with handbags filled with essentials for the anticipated day. We loaded them in the van one by one. We were going on a new adventure. Petra, the coordinator, would consider relocating to Ilhabela to lead the work on the island for Lar Feliz.

"What do you think of that, Petra?" I asked with a giggle.

At a gas stop, a brochure with a woman on the beach was handed to us. A tall young man with creamy skin wearing colorful beach pants also stood close by the van.

"There also might be one of those for you. Look!" Adriana elbowed Petra while laughing into her hands. Petra didn't say a word but only giggled good-naturedly. Only God knew. Maybe it would work out for her this time. Hope twinkled in her eyes.

"If it would be like that brochure, then indeed it would just be fantastic!" Petra said quietly, as everyone smiled and laughed.

Petra, who had done an amazing job at Lar Feliz in Jaguariúna, felt that her time there was done. She was thinking of moving on. She had been torn between the idea of starting a clinic for pregnant teens in Posse or coming to Ilhabela.

After a ten-hour road trip that seemed to drag on with many stops, we finally arrived at the line to get on the ferry and the island. A refreshing wind brushed over us, and everything around was tranquil. The line for the big ferry moved along continually as the van edged closer to the front of the line. Soon, it was our turn to pull on to the long flat boat that appeared to have endless room on it. Once full, it tugged along at a slow pace to bring everyone from Sao Sabastion to Ilhabela.

We arrived an hour and a half early and were on our feet, stretching. We drove close to the building, where we were to meet with the current leader of the shelter.

"Let's find some place to eat!" said Rodolfo, one of the directors of Lar Feliz. Rodolfo had a gift for finding the best spots with the best food and the best prices.

There was a little restaurant down the road that had just enough room for everyone to sit. The special was "Fresh Catch of the Day!"

"I'll have that!" I said as I nudged Paul. If on an island, there was nothing better to eat than fresh fish. A few of us ordered fish, and some got steak. Every executive lunch plate was the same price. Then we all ordered drinks. A few of us had carbonated water; some had soda; and some had orange juice without sugar or water added. Each lunch plate began with a small salad that the waiter brought out almost immediately with all the drinks.

We had a nice lunch, and we discussed over lunch how we hoped that things would go. This was a "spy out the land" sort of trip. Nothing was certain, and we hadn't signed any contract yet. It was a new open door, but was it the right door? This we would have to see for ourselves as we visited the children's home. It would be the city officials who would decide who would be taking it on. It was a new policy that promoted healthy competition to bring about the best results.

After lunch, we prepared to go by the office of the city officials; and then we could ask to see the children's home. As it was a tiny space with a winding set of stairs, only five were able to come in.

"If you would like to see the children's home, we can arrange it for you," the secretary said.

"Yes, we would like to see it," Pastor Paul said.

The neighborhood was quiet at the time. A lonely bus stop was in front of a quaint green house built atop a hill. Behind the smaller house was a larger house that had an attractive balcony where one could view the whole island. There were no children in sight. Suddenly, a van drove away quickly with all the children on it as well as a monitor.

"At our home, the children aren't allowed any visitors," the young coordinator simply said. She brushed away her long sandy hair from her oval green eyes. Clothed in a simple tie-dye shirt and pants with a wild multicolored print, she nimbly climbed the winding stairs.

"Let's go!" She waved toward a small winding staircase that led to the children's home. We entered the living room; and everything smelled clean with the scent of rubbing alcohol, which was commonly used to clean the surfaces and the windows. Along the corridor revealed rows of tiny bedrooms where each dormitory was. At the end was one cluttered bathroom, the unlocked door fastened shut with only a string. It was the only one for a whole house of people!

Upon entering the kitchen, we saw a tiny workspace with two large refrigerators and an industrial-sized stove. The pantry was behind an old, thin curtain with the corner wrapped around a nail to reveal boxes of pasta, canned vegetables, cartons of milk, and a cat named Romeo on the top shelf.

"He keeps the mice away!" someone said.

"He has got to go!" Petra said. "No cats allowed in the kitchen!"

The bright sun painted the waters of the sea with a pink glow as the day ended. The whole team of Lar Feliz felt satisfied at the end of the cool day. This was a wonderful opportunity, and we should not let it slip through our fingers. After a quick swim in the chilly, winter waters, we sat at a coffee shop to discuss details.

"Would you be able to manage things on your own?" Pastor Paul asked Petra. "How will you feel if there is a riot among the teen boys, for example, and we are not able to come right away to solve it."

They sat around the picnic table thinking quietly. Petra had been a sergeant in the royal Dutch army, and she was a leader who could oversee a variety of conflicts and problems. Would this be a position that she could manage on her own? The drive from Holambra to the island was around six hours, depending on the traffic and the line to get on the ferry.

"Yes!" Petra nodded her head. "I think I can do it."

"Wait a minute!" Veronica shouted from a distance. Veronica was the psychologist who attended the children of the project in Jaguariúna. She had helped many children grow leaps and bounds with the therapy needed to resolve the issues of adjusting to new families. She had a big heart of love for children and adolescents alike.

"I will stay with you, Petra! I will relocate and work with you here as the psychologist on the technical team." Veronica walked briskly from the beach with a towel wrapped around her.

We decided together to take on the new shelter at Ilhabela. Lar Feliz reached its arms out to a new location. The two courageous friends would stay and work together to run the children's project on the beautiful island. It might not always be the smooth course that they had hoped for, but the two women would learn and embark on a new, challenging adventure in a beautiful place that seemed to the traveler like paradise.

For Petra, the dream of starting a project in Posse was now put aside for a new and amazing opportunity.

Posse had decided to go in a different direction. Paul and the technical team talked around the dining room table with two of the men from the children's counsel. A new organization would take on the task of starting a new children's home—on the ranch of the current mayor, no less. An opening ceremony would take place on October 31.

The public calling had served its purpose, and Posse would begin something else without the help or work of Lar Feliz. The conclusion of our work came, though the decision left sadness in its wake. For years, we had served Posse. The children from their town had mostly grown up in Jaguariúna. Now, they would have to uproot and move to a new place with a new team of workers and psychologists. The planning had the wheels turning in all the minds of the technical team. Hopefully, a smooth transition would take place according to plan.

It was a bright, sunny day when a large bus owned by the city came to take the children to their new home. It arrived after lunch time, and the children were allowed to take all their belongings that they had accumulated throughout the years—any toys, clothing, and various pairs of shoes would be permitted.

"Can I bring my new puppy?" a teen boy asked Pastor Paul. Occasionally, a female dog would come and have a litter of puppies at the farm. It was not unusual for the children to choose one that they could keep. The pups were usually "viralatas," or mixed breeds; but they were lovable and adorable, especially when small.

"Yes, as long as it is okay for the new home!" Pastor Paul replied.

They sat down in the dining hall for their last meal together, and a small photo album with their pictures of growing up at Lar Feliz was presented to each one by Pastor Paul.

Bia smiled and produced tears. She was almost eighteen, and she had arrived as a curly haired toddler full of fun and mischief when she was only two years old. Though she was a handful at times, she had changed and developed in a beautiful way. She had grown.

It was 11:45, and they each walked up the big hill toward the parking lot on the outside of the gate. Rodolfo held the smallest little blonde girl, and Rodrigo gathered all the technical papers and medicines in a Ziplock bag. They waited. The bus was late as the time of pick-up had passed one hour. Paul called the new home, and no one answered.

I peered down the road over the hill from where the bus would come. My arms ached from holding a little one. What could have happened? Finally, an hour and a half later, a mystery bus arrived with only a driver and no staff.

"That can't be!" said Rodrigo holding onto the papers and bottles of medication. "I will not send these children without the care of an adult! They might throw their medication out the window!"

It seemed to all the staff at Lar Feliz an ominous start. Was it possible that they had changed their minds? Paul continued to call the new president of the organization that would take over for Lar Feliz in Posse.

Finally, someone answered and simply said, "We are still waiting for the bus!"
"The bus is already here!" Paul exclaimed.

The bus had come directly to Lar Feliz without picking up any staff members. We waited until the staff could come in a separate car of their own. One or two adults would ride on the bus, and three little ones would ride along in the car.

After they hurriedly arrived, it was time for them to load all the kids and their belongings. We hugged and brushed away tears as each one said their emotional goodbyes. The only happy face in the crowd was the mischievous teenage boy bringing his new puppy.

Once they were gone and we waved goodbye, Paul and I received an invitation to the grand opening of the new home, which would take place on October 31 in the evening.

"That is a bad sign!" I later told Paul at home. "Who would open a home on Halloween night?"

It was a clear afternoon when we set out to participate in the opening of the new children's home in Posse named "Mother Maria" after the mayor's mother. The beautiful, large home, located in the city center, was hidden off the main street by a long, narrow lane. As we pulled down the driveway, suddenly the clouds opened; and the rain poured furiously. The new unpaved parking lot was filled with all kinds of cars parked in complete disorder. Paul and I had forgotten our umbrella and ran like the others to the veranda of the house, where we could take shelter from the rain. A hundred muddy footprints tracked the hall in the doorway as people unfortunately had no way of cleaning the bottoms of their shoes, and there was no rug in sight.

The play area had games in boxes and cartons of scissors and crayons. There were dolls and little cars and balls placed on the shelves next to tiny chairs. Along the ceiling and the hallway were rows of immaculate windows. My thoughts returned to a time when one of the naughty boys had broken the windows at the dining hall by throwing pebbles one by one. When asked why, he had simply replied, "It was fun!"

Through the years, serving Posse had not always been easy; so, it was with smiles and mixed feelings that we participated in the event. We were not there to advise, only to bless, pray, and give our well-wishes.

At that moment, the mayor got up to speak. The large ranch house was the second home of his family. He had invested a part of his heart in this children's home. He told about their dreams to open their very own children's home. It was his passion to do so, as well as the social worker of the town.

"It was their dream," I whispered.

It was something they, as a town, had longed for. It was not anything personal against Lar Feliz. There did not seem to be anything political about it. It was simply their longing to have their own children's home close by the families. The large hall was filled with all kinds of people who were eager to roll up their sleeves and help.

At that moment, the mayor directed his attention to Paul and me.

"We want to thank Pastor Paul and Lar Feliz for all of their years of collaborating with us," he said with a nod. "Now is our time to build our own home for the good of our community! I know the people of Posse—how good they are—and I know that they will always be there to help where needed."

The inauguration celebration was closed with a prayer—first by the Catholic padre and then by a pastor of the Assembly of God church in town.

"Let's go home!" I whispered to Paul.

"No, let's go out for a bite to eat. How about pizza?"

We slipped out the back door with barely a wave goodbye as the rest gathered around the table where there were food and drinks and flowers that were being given away to individuals.

We left with rested minds that our work at Posse was over and done. A short thank you was given by the political members that barely covered all the struggle, blood, sweat, tears, and suffering that we had endured through the years of demanding work. We did not take care of the children to receive the thanks and praise of men. We did it out of love for God and all the young lives that had passed through.

The towns of Posse and Jaguariúna would now be separated in the care of the children, like two brothers who had outgrown one another. Posse would move on, developing their own home, facing very new and difficult challenges of being in the town center. Lar Feliz would go through all kinds of changes in workers and policies, but it would not only continue to survive—it would thrive. It was a new day.

Six months later, we heard how difficult the home in Posse was becoming; but we would continue, steadfast in the decision of separating. God would provide. The future, though unseen, was very bright!

## CHAPTER 31
# A Feast

*"Then he said unto them, 'Go your way, eat the fat, and drink the sweet, and send portions unto them for whom nothing is prepared: for this day is holy unto our Lord: neither be ye sorry; for the joy of the LORD is your strength.'"*

Nehemiah 8:10

## Jaguariúna, Lar Feliz
Christmas time

The dining room was exquisitely decorated with paper streamers; a fat Christmas tree; and even a friendly, life-sized Santa in the corner. Lights around the windows erratically blinked on and off as delicious smells filled the room together with the tinkling of laughter of workers slowly filing in. The tables formed a giant "U," each place set with red and white napkins and cutlery.

"Come in, everyone! It is about time for our Christmas party to begin," Paul said as the workers began to slowly file in.

The decorations for the party and the care in the handmade ornaments made everyone feel special. A woman touched the ornaments of the tree as she recognized they were made by the children. Toward the front, a giant food table held rectangular pans of steaming hot food covered by flat lids.

Rice, beans, potato salad, lasagna, and pork with fruits were on the menu today. Nothing but the best for those who gave their all to the children at Lar Feliz. The atmosphere of joy continued to grow as Tía Selma came in last with the baby house staff pushing some buggies of sleeping babies.

Most of the children had gone to different homes for Christmas with relatives, friends, or, when possible, their own parents. During this special time of year, most children wanted to celebrate at home. Unfortunately, every year, there were some left behind with nowhere to go. For those who stayed behind for the holidays at Lar Feliz, there would be special meals, gifts, and sweets to try to make up for what was missed.

Pastor Paul stood up. "Let's have a word of prayer before we start; and after the meal, we will have our chocolate gift exchange!" A few chuckles were heard as one man elbowed someone next to him, a knowing grin directed toward the table of odd-sized gifts.

A hush entered the room as they all quieted and prayed together. "Father God, I thank You for this past year at Lar Feliz and how You have provided for so many lives in so many miraculous ways. We just want to say thank You for all that You do for us. Thank You for all Your love for us! Thank You for the food. Amen!"

"Amen" echoed throughout the room with different voices.

"Let's eat!"

Each worker filed in line, took a glass plate from the stack, and filled it with heaping piles of food. There was something for everyone's taste, including salads and puddings for dessert. Some of the strong men even went back for seconds, and no one dared to diet. Lar Feliz had a very good reputation for having wonderful food. There were even two officials from Posse who came every week without fail for lunch.

Some cooks simply cooked, and there were those who did it with love. There were cooks who could cook love right into the food! It was easy to see the difference; and the children grew and thrived when eating good, healthy food.

As the eating began to slow down and the plates were washed and stacked by the sink, Sonia, the secretary, walked along with a small bowl holding bits of paper with numbers written on it. Each staff person in turn picked a number, quickly unfolding it with delight in their eyes. Soon, the fun would begin.

"Number one," Paul yelled above the noise of voices around the table.

"Me!"

One of the workers from the girls' home ran to the front to inspect the gift table. After carefully looking up and down, she decided on the biggest box with its blue and white paper. She ran back to her seat.

"Next! Number two!" Paul shouted. "Now, you can either take away the first present from Maria, or you can choose a new one if you like. It's up to you!"

Aline suddenly raised her hand and then predictably went to take Maria's large gift in front of her on the table. The whole room erupted in laughter as poor Maria had to go to the front to choose another gift. She found an expensive-looking gift bag with a high-quality brand of chocolate. She was safe for now from the next one who could either choose one of the gifts that had been taken or pick a new gift from the table.

On and on it went until everyone had a gift sitting in front of them on the table. They all hoped for the best as they unwrapped their chocolate gifts. No one wanted any of the "cheap chocolate"—as Isa and Jeremy had called it—that was made in Brazil and melted rapidly.

Shouts and laughter filled the room as everyone unmasked their gifts of chocolate. Some of the packages had been disguised by using paper and large empty boxes, but they were holding only a tiny box of chocolate inside. The gift bags were usually always a win. Even though small, they were true to their content. The party was a grand success—a favorite among all.

As I looked around the room filled with smiles and hugs from the workers, a sadness filled my heart. "The only constant that we have in this life is that things are always changing. We must adapt to change, and we must embrace change though it is not always easy," I had shared at a conference not long ago about the new Brazilian laws regarding children's shelters. I had said those words with such confidence at the time, but putting them into practice was always so much harder than theory. At the end of the year, 50 percent of these very workers would be laid off and would have to look for jobs elsewhere.

## CHAPTER 32
# At Home in Paradise

*"The very nature of paradise is that it will be lost."*[16]

—Melissa Coleman

Paul pulled our family car over to the exit by a bakery where Cristiane, the social worker, was waiting at the curb. Paul and I got out of the car to help her put her luggage into the trunk. Even though the three of us would only be spending a few days in Ilhabela, the trunk and part of the back seat were full. We were bringing Tupperware containers filled with art supplies, boxes of freshly baked raisin breads to sell, fresh pillows and blankets because the ones at the cheap hotel had a faint odor, beach towels, and shoes. We got out fresh bottles of water before starting off on the six-hour journey—if the line for the ferry was short—to reach the beautiful island called Ilhabela.

We listened to a steady stream of gospel music as Paul drove along. He intermittently had discussions with Cristiane, who leaned forward from the back seat. They had some important things to discuss about the meetings that were ahead, and they wanted to be prepared. Lar Feliz was opening its arms to a new location on the island, and we would manage two children's homes. The farm in Jaguariúna would continue the same way, only with a smaller number of children; and we would manage—from a distance—a

---

16   Melissa Coleman, *This Life is in Your Hands* (New York: HarperCollins, April, 10 2012).

house in town at Ilhabela. The home in Jaguariúna had drastically shrunk in size after the city of Santo Antonio de Posse no longer required our services and decided to start a new home in their own city.

A lot of the workers at Lar Feliz would be temporarily laid off, until the numbers of children attending would grow again. A few of the staff would be able to work on the island. Coming once a month, we would discuss the problems, get to know the children and the area, and bring any supplies that were needed for the staff leaders, Petra and Veronica.

It was my dream job! Being a volunteer, I could create what I would do according to the present need. I had much more flexibility, which I had craved in the past years of leading the baby house. Surprisingly, I found the teens and children at the home very eager to do arts and crafts. I planned activities with them to sit at the table making things, painting pictures, and even baking cookies. I was able to pass on the passion to create to the naturally gifted children living on the island. Being well-behaved and attentive, the small children and teenagers listened to me and followed instructions carefully. Their openness shined through their eyes as they sang along together to the gospel music while using their artistic talents. They made exquisite things to cherish, like colorful decorations for their Christmas tree and painted pictures of the sea that were taped and hung on the wall behind their breakfast table.

During free time, Paul and I sipped drinks at the beach; and then at night, we shared meals together at a restaurant, where we discussed how everything was going. In the afternoons, when the children were mostly at school, I swam like a fish in the ocean—my happy place—where stress and worry plunged to the bottom of the sea. I meditated on Bible verses and painted water-color pictures of the scenery on the island with beautiful shades of blue green.

Paul had the most difficult task of the two of us, holding long meetings where everyone must be heard from. Doing children's work was not for the weak but for the warrior with sharpened sword, figuratively. One had to be prepared to defend the rights of the children, while at the same time, keeping the home functioning flawlessly with no lump in the batter.

The administration that oversaw the spending of funds for the children's project would need a lot of paperwork showing where each amount of money was being sent. They had lots of money they said could be used, but they were misers when it came to buying food and supplies for the children. Trying to get the extra money needed was like taking a bone from a dog. It was challenging and nerve-wracking but, in the end, possible. Everything needed to have an explanation—from buying a new pair of shoes to packages of instant soup. It was a lot of extra work for everyone involved. When Petra had to do grocery shopping, she needed to be her own accountant at the end, remembering the codes and making sure that everything added up in the budget.

"Well, we can always ask for donations!" Paul said when referring to getting new toys and school supplies. In Jaguariúna, we had the support of our community, including churches of all denominations, schools, clubs, and individuals. Whenever something was needed—whether it be diapers, milk powder, shoes, or clothing for school—everything was supplied. Lar Feliz had a good name and a good reputation in Jaguariúna; but in Ilhabela, we were newcomers.

"No, we don't ask for donations!" the city officials said.

There was a lot to learn in working with the new city and their ways, which were so different from what we had been used to.

Paradise on an island wouldn't be complete without a few challenges here and there, but there were more things about to go wrong.

"It's normal to have a little bit of tension at work; after all, we have different viewpoints," I told Rodrigo, the psychologist who worked at Lar Feliz in Jaguariúna.

The slogan on the back of the Lar Feliz uniform read, "Lar Feliz, because God loves the children." It was the starting point of everyone who worked at Lar Feliz—loving kids. There were times when the children were not easy to love, but they were always loved by God. Unfortunately, there were many variations on *how* to demonstrate that love. Through these differences of opinions came serious disagreements.

In Brazil, there was often a fluid flow of thoughts and practices and color instead of black and white. Ideas and laws could change overnight. Untried theories were put into practice until they proved not worthy of use, and everything changed again.

Petra had settled into her home in the top apartment of the cozy green house that was shelter for ten children. On a clear day, the sun gave a beautiful view of the mountains and beach. She brought only a few essentials, clothing, some Dutch teacups, and her sewing machine. She breathed in the fresh air, and she welcomed the change of scenery. It was a town of new beginnings for her. She was like a beautiful Dutch swan who, without a mate, continued to swim on alone to her given destination. Her heart had an empty place as she longed for a mate to join her.

Veronica, her friend who came to work with her, had very different points of view on almost everything going on at the project. As a Brazilian woman who had worked full time as a child's psychologist, she went beyond expectations; and she saw many children healed and liberated from their past. The key to therapy was in unraveling the wrong thoughts to make room for the new ones. She didn't give up until she saw some results.

The surroundings of the quaint green house that were still during the day took on a new life as soon as the sun set—misery revealed in the simple neighborhood that bad dreams were made of. It turned out that the bus stop was, in fact, a meeting point for the youth to buy and sell drugs. A thousand bikes were ridden by teenage boys speeding by without any real place to go. In their idleness, they usually found trouble. In Brazil, that meant drugs. The bright future was clouded by poverty, lack of education, and a low salary that barely bought a meal. The youth turned to a quick fix—selling drugs was quick money. They couldn't see past the fog obstructing their view of productivity, peace, prosperity, and a family that was whole. They chose to dive headlong into the dark abyss that took years to climb out of. Everyone in Brazil knew someone who had an addiction problem. It was everywhere. The promise of the politicians was like an uncashed check that did little to provide for their economic needs.

It had been a hard day when Isa and Jeremy said, "We aren't staying in Brazil. There is nothing for us here."

It was decided then that when they became of age, our own children would move to the USA, where they could begin their future. They could make money and build dreams that weren't achievable in Brazil for the young people of the day. They deeply loved Brazil—the beaches, the fresh baked buns, the barbecues, and the sense of humor of the delightful people—but it wasn't enough to make them stay. For me, it was a continuing ache not having our children living in Brazil; but Isa and Jeremy thrived and flourished in the US in a way that would never have been possible living their adult lives with their parents. As I observed the youth struggling in Brazil to find their place, it was at least one consolation that our own adult children were no longer living here. They had made the right choice, and they were living their best lives.

As we gathered around the table for dinner at a Mexican restaurant called Kalango, the discussion was heated and then peaceful, like waves coming and going in a coming storm.

"We cannot continue our children's home at that house in that kind of neighborhood," we said in agreement.

There was just no way of helping teenagers fight their own demons with drugs while being in proximity to on-going drug trafficking.

"We must go to the city officials and tell them what we want! We will go talk to Dona Nilse," Paul said as the plan of action for the very near future. Paul looked at his agenda on the cell phone and attempted to make an appointment with her.

The workers of the mayor's office at Ilhabela worked long hours, sometimes until 9:00 at night. They slept in; and then they worked later, unlike the Brazilians of rural areas who got up with the sun and worked until six. Both groups worked very hard to better their nation. Sometimes, they had a big salary; and sometimes, they didn't. But they truly did their best work. Even though we were only six hours away at Ilhabela, it was a completely different world from Holambra. There was a totally different way of doing things. We had to start learning everything all over again.

"Dona Nilse, we need to have a meeting before we drive home to Holambra. It is very important! Can you please give us an hour of your time?"

Paul sounded very convincing on the phone; and Dona Nilse, true to her word, made an appointment with us and the mayor for the following afternoon at 2:00.

The following day, the team members were served some weak herbal tea as we waited at the reception.

"Can I have some water, please?" I asked.

It was too hot for tea. The hour passed, and we continued to wait as it was nearly 4:00.

"The mayor had some things come up, but now he will see you," said the secretary.

"Two hours late," Petra said. (The Dutch are the most punctual in the world.)

I had been a little late in my life but never two hours late for any appointment. That was very late, but it seemed common enough that the workers there didn't seem to notice.

The mayor ushered us into his office with a big smile. He had gifts for the women on the team, as well as polo shirts for Paul and me.

"I am so glad that you are here and serving the children on this island," he said.

The mayor was from a Baptist background, so Paul suggested sharing a Scripture and prayer together. The mayor bowed his head and was grateful.

After the brief meeting with the officials, the decision was made that the local government would supply the funds for Lar Feliz to purchase a new home, where the children would live. The following month, I discovered that the budget reached higher than I had ever known. Paul and I went with Dona Nilse and the technical team to shop for the very best house. I saw stylish beautiful homes on the beach that I would love one day for myself, but they weren't appropriate for a house filled with children of all ages. Finally, close to the school on one side and the beach on the other, we found the right place.

## CHAPTER 33
# Shelter or Home

*"Home is the place where, when you have to go there, they have to take you in."*[17]

—Robert Frost

As we walked together through the green house, I carefully pointed out some things to Dona Nilse.

"The living room is so small. They can't do much there but watch television. At our home in Jaguariúna, the children barely watch it at all! Look at the dining table there. It is so small that only half of the household can sit at it at a time! Wouldn't it be nice if everyone could eat together?"

As I pointed out a few of these things to her, she nodded. It gave her a new perspective and a goal to achieve.

The yard at the tiny green house, which was the size of a kitchen table, only had a small swing set; so, the children mainly sat inside when not in school.

"Imagine if the children had a swimming pool. How refreshing that would be for them!" I gave her my opinion, and Dona Nilse liked my ideas.

The next day, we went on an adventure to see prospective homes. We discovered the very rich who resided at Ilhabela, whereas before, we only saw the poor and desperate streets. The difference of the neighborhoods was vast indeed. Paul and I went with Dona Nilse and the technical team to shop for

---

17  Robert Frost, *The Death of the Hired Man*, lines 122-23.

the very best house. I saw stylish beautiful homes on the beach that I would love one day for myself, but they weren't appropriate for a house filled with children of all ages.

"How much did you say this one cost?" Paul asked while we looked at an out-of-the-way property with red flowers growing on the path. It was breathtakingly luxurious, and it checked all the boxes.

"One million!" Dona Nilse said. "It is a little bit out of the way, though, for the children's home. We should look at one closer to the school."

Finally, we found a newer home close by the school, the hospital, and the grocery store. And most importantly, it was within walking distance of the beach!

Yeah! I knew what I would do during my free time!

Petra and Veronica continued to work very hard at the new children's home, which was in constant motion of change. There were renovations that needed to be done; the garden needed to be kept nice; workers came and went; and many new children arrived until the home was filled. They hardly took any time off and devoted themselves completely to Lar Feliz, Ilhabela.

When we called Petra to check on how she was doing, she said that she continued to feel the lonely ache of missing her friends back in Jaguariúna; and she felt out of place, too. She talked about other dreams which she longed to pursue but was unable because of the heavy responsibility of running the home.

Veronica had invited her to a home group of a life-giving church called "Bola de Neve" or "The Snowball Church." As there wasn't any snow in Brazil, it was probably named because it grew like a snowball, rolling down a hill, eventually growing bigger and bigger.

At the home group and church, she met a kindhearted man named Franklin. He had a bright smile and bronzed skin. He loved the island and was a great sportsman. He loved the Lord Jesus and shined His light everywhere he went, and he captured Petra's heart.

He seemed to like her, too; but after they prayed, it seemed best to wait.

"Only be led by His peace," they were told by their pastors.

Everything had its own perfect time. Still, they kept contact and became very good friends.

As Lar Feliz Ilhabela continued to grow and prosper, a second home was opened to keep up with all the children coming. It was decided to rent a property across the street to make room for more children. There were whole families of siblings being sent to the home. The brothers and sisters were kept together and were encouraged to keep in contact, strengthening the bond that was in existence. It grew so much that the neighbors began to complain of the noise.

"Maybe we can bake her a cake," I said to the cook, laughing as the neighbor woman yelled at Petra coming in on her bike.

"She would believe that it had been poisoned, I'm afraid," Petra said.

They tried to keep the children quiet in the once peaceful street of the residential neighborhood, but it was to no avail. They were in the city, and the little boys especially needed something to do.

As Samuel, a young boy from the project, rode his bike in a figure eight for the thirtieth time, he nearly ran over a baby.

"Stop!" yelled the monitor.

When he did stop riding his bike in the small area, his idle mind thought up something else mischievous to do instead. The home was full.

"It's your turn," I said as I rolled out the remainder of the cookie dough on a wooden table that was generously covered in flour.

A little girl with two brown ponytails chose a cookie cutter the shape of a hand and pressed down with all her might.

"That will do," I said with a gentle smile.

The Christmas cookies were placed on a round pizza pan and put into the hot oven.

"Yum," I said as we took a taste of the warm cookies during the coffee time.

"What is different? There is something different in the taste of these cookies," one of the women workers said.

"It's my grandmother's recipe, and it uses butter." I showed a small card with my grandmother's recipe.

"That's it! I tasted the butter. What beautiful and tasty cookies they are!"

"I will give you all the recipe! They are easy to make and so much fun for the children!"

I had found a new home. On this island, everything seemed to be at a slower pace. People were friendly and shared coffee and meals together.

"When are you coming back?" they asked as we packed our car to go.

"Hopefully soon!" I said, looking forward to visiting often.

At times, I even felt that I could live there.

# Rolled Cookies
## From the Kitchen of Hazel Willa Perry

- 2 cups flour
- 1 ½ tsp. baking powder
- ½ tsp. salt
- ½ cup butter
- ¾ cup sugar
- 1 egg
- 1 Tbsp. milk
- 1 tsp. vanilla
- 1 Tbsp. sugar and ¼ tsp. cinnamon to sprinkle on top

## Directions:

1. Cream butter and sugar.
2. Add egg and beat.
3. Stir in vanilla and milk.
4. Add dry ingredients.
5. Chill dough.
6. Roll thin.
7. Bake at 400 degrees for six to ten minutes.

## CHAPTER 34
# It's All a Game

*"The game is not over until it is."*[18]

—Dwight York

As I hurriedly drove home from the project, I thought I would stop at the grocery store at the corner near where we lived. There weren't any cars in the parking lot, and it was closed in the middle of the day. Like a scene from the apocalypse, the streets that were usually buzzing were completely empty; and the stores and the schools were closed. Today was the day that the Brazilian team played in the tournament of the World Cup. Everyone was at home watching.

I had just made it home, clad in my Brazilian soccer shirt, when I heard the sports announcer on the television loudly shout in Portuguese, "Goal!"

"For us or for them?" I asked as I moved quickly into the living room.

"Who do you think?" Paul said.

"Braaaaaaaaaaaazil!" came the next loud announcement.

Brazil was ahead but maybe not for long.

The days when Brazil played were like none that I had ever seen. Everyone, whether they liked soccer or not, stopped what they were doing and watched and rooted along. The true-to-life heroes, many times from the slums of Sao

---

18   Dwight Yorke, *Born to Score* (London, Macmillan, 2009).

Paulo or Rio de Janeiro, became multi-millionaires who gave to charities and started new trends in hair styles.

Every little boy and a few girls had that dream. "If only I practice and am good enough, my life will change; and I will become rich." At Lar Feliz, our sand bottomed soccer field was in use every day with barefooted children attempting to make a goal.

In the time of Pelé—the most famous player in Brazil—a nation was changed and a dictatorship overthrown because of a World Cup win. Brazil grew up into a democracy when the people realized that they had a part on the world stage. It was, in a way, the reason that soccer, or *futebol*, was the most important element of the culture. Time went on. And as the democracy began to take shape, though the system was still mind-boggling, schools were developed; and children often grew up and went to college.

When Brazil lost to Germany while hosting the World Cup that year, many intellectuals in Brazil gave their two cents that the nation no longer revolved around a soccer game. Even so, the love affair that the Brazilians had with soccer is far from over.

One January, my brother, Jason, came to visit with his wife, Jen, and daughters, Morgan and Madison. Soccer was their beloved sport, and Jason coached it for years for the girls' teams. For fun, they decided to challenge the Lar Feliz little boys to an easy match on a full-sized field. There were boys of all sizes playing; and under the sweltering Brazilian sun, they could run for hours on end. They owned one pair of soccer shoes between them, so they shared. One little boy used a shoe on his left foot, and another little boy used it on his right foot; and they took turns among the whole team who would use the shoe next. My brother's team lost 0-6, to his shock.

"Those boys have talent and potential," he said.

Two of the boys from Lar Feliz did grow up with a shot at playing professionally on the Brazilian team. When I asked one of the boys, Felipe, why he didn't stay with it, he answered that the cost was just too high.

"The only thing that we could think about was *futebol*, nothing else," he said. "No relationships, no family, no other interests, no religion. Soccer had to be our whole world and nothing else."

His brother Rian also said, "Brazil will always love soccer. You know why? It's because we have something in common with the other nations of the world. We can kick a ball and make a goal."

Reality television was already popular in Brazil long before it came to be anywhere else; and there was one particular game show called "Who Will Tell the Truth?" that wrecked several families in one episode. Nothing would ever be the same again, and the one who suffered the most was a little girl named Suzana.

One evening, the game show came on with a very beautiful and pregnant young woman who was about to point out the father of her unborn child—a man who seemed to be upstanding in society. Amidst the outrage and sickening scenes, a family was lost. Afterward, the young woman chose to live, homeless, alone on the streets. She gave birth to her daughter, who learned to fend for herself at a young age.

Suzana came to Lar Feliz at six years old. She had honey-colored brown eyes and a sweet, sincere smile that undid me. It all started off fine until the fits of crisis began. She would yell and scream and cry, and there was nothing that would console her. She talked a lot of trash for a young girl, which led us to believe that her innocence had been stolen, possibly on the streets where she had lived. Many times, group activities with her ended in disaster when things didn't go as she liked. One time, while painting, she covered every surface in black gauche when I turned my back for only a few minutes.

It was challenging, but underneath the shattered pieces of her inner being was a heart. She still had courage to love. She loved animals and babies, and she loved people, too. In time, after a lot of therapy and medication, she could control herself and stay calm. She accepted Jesus, and she is loved by her Savior. She had a future and a chance to have a normal life someday. It was our dream for her to be placed for adoption in a new family. One day in the future it may happen; but until it does, she has family at Lar Feliz.

CHAPTER 35

## School Break

*"The voice of rejoicing and salvation is in the tabernacles of the righteous: the right hand of the LORD doeth valiantly."*

Psalm 118:15

### Lar Feliz, Jaguariúna
January 2019

The new staff t-shirts had been ordered in orange with bold black letters that read, "Camp Lar Feliz 2019" with the little house logo on the front. Rodrigo, the psychologist, and Daiane, the social worker, sat in the office with Pastor Paul as they organized the final details for the summer vacation weeks ahead. It was time for Lar Feliz to try something new.

The month before we had to let about 50 percent of the staff go. They left with severance pay that would help them in the months ahead of finding a new job. For most, the time and experience at Lar Feliz had opened new doors of opportunity for the workers who had to leave. As the children's homes shrank down in number, the staff who were left caught a new vision of what could take place during the summer break from school. The idea was to use their resources as a summer camp for children of needy neighborhoods.

Using the network they had, they were able to arrange for children of all ages to come and spend a week at Lar Feliz, where they would participate in all sorts of activities—both educational and fun. They would paint a picture with Professor Ever, do arts and crafts with Tía Jill, swim in the pool, have games, and, lastly, take a trip to the shopping mall. Each week, a different age group would come and have a wonderful time. They would return home to their families refreshed and happy.

"Do you live here, Miquel?" Robert asked.

"Yes, I do. What of it?"

"I wish that I could live here, too! Lar Feliz is a wonderful place!" Robert said.

In that moment, I nudged Rodrigo. "Did you hear what they said?"

"I did. That's amazing, isn't it?" Rodrigo said.

"It is so nice to feel appreciated!"

The children who stayed for only a week were capable of being obedient and kind to each other. It was a rare occasion if there was an argument among them. It was a new time and season for Lar Feliz in Jaguariúna. After all the hard years of struggle, we were in a season of rest. Just as the rusty chain on a bicycle gets oiled, so we were able to fix some things and glide effortlessly ahead as we prepared for the future years.

We loaded up all the teenagers in the rented micro-bus. All the staff were clad with orange t-shirts that read "Lar Feliz" on the front. The teens were from a needy neighborhood and had never ventured out to the big city of Campinas. Every eye was glued to the window, enjoying the new view. After we rode on the highway for about forty minutes, we pulled into the lot behind the Shopping Parque Dom Pedro—the largest shopping mall in South America. We quietly exited and turned to see a brightly decorated entrance.

"We're here! Let's gather around," Pastor Paul said. "Each one of you will have two hundred reais to spend on new clothes, and that includes new shoes. Use it well! After shopping, we will all meet at McDonald's."

It was the perfect day of giving. Each child and teen was accompanied by a staff volunteer, who helped them pick out clothes at a Brazilian clothing store.

A few hours passed. It was time to check out. All the clothes and the shoes were rung up at the cash register.

"Give me the bill," Paul said as he reached for his credit card to pay. "Now let's go have a Big Mac!"

After all the calculations were made, the grand total for all the children at summer camp to buy new clothes came to twelve thousand reais, or about $2,000, depending on the current exchange rate. The money was provided by the Bank of Brazil, who supported the summer program. It was a season of rest. It was a season of giving.

When the summer camp was over and the last bus of children rolled down the dirt road back to the city, Lar Feliz was still once again. The children were shifted to a few of the homes located at the farm, and the rest of the buildings remained empty and unused. The number of children was down to a mere twenty-five; before, the number had stayed at around fifty. The staff hall was a tranquil place, and a handful of staff took their meal at one long table. Before, the noise of laughter and clanging plates being washed drowned out conversation. Times had changed, but some things remained the same. The food was as delicious as ever with rice, beans, fried chicken, salad, limeade, and fresh fruit for dessert.

## CHAPTER 36
# God is Love

*"Grace changes everything, even how you believe."*[19]

—Erich Engler

"All is fair in love and war,"[20] as well as in church-planting. So, it would seem. Except in the end, it really wasn't. There is nothing that breaks a pastor's heart more than preaching to a half-empty church. Rather than being happy with the people who came, we tended to focus on the ones who didn't come to church; and we wondered why.

In 2015, Paul and I and the other pastors, Rodolfo and Andressa from our congregation, experienced a refreshing new revelation of grace. Near to burn out working many hours at Lar Feliz, we attended a conference with Marcel and Cody Gaasenbeek that would forever change our perspective.

While listening to Marcel's teachings on the love of God, the veil of the fear of man was removed from my heart. The vision and our love for Jesus was made new. Gone were the self-righteous, dead works that were like dirty rags. We had received a fresh vision of God's grace. Instead of burning out, we received a fresh fire from the Holy Spirit, a zeal, and a passion for God's Word. God made a noticeable difference in our lives;

---

19  Erich Engler, "Next Level Faith" (sermon), Rhema Bible Church, South Africa, December 4, 2023.
20  John Lyly, *Euphues: The Anatomy of Wit* (London, 1578).

and in the next year, we established a new church called Community of the New and the Free.

During that time, I received victory in many areas in my life after the simple grace conference, where the undying love of Jesus was revealed to us in a fresh way! I realized that I was loved deeply by Jesus, which caused a freedom in my other relationships, including my marriage with Paul. Bible study became my favorite pastime. When I opened the Word, reading by the power of the Holy Spirit through the glasses of grace, everything became new. I began to see the fulfillment of God's promises and the correlation between the Old and New Testaments.

A few years prior, Paul had begun to have constant headaches and tiredness; and he feared that he might be dying. As he would talk to me about it to prepare me, I gave him my response.

"No, you're not! I won't let you! Let's change the subject."

We visited the doctors, and nothing was found wrong. After Paul received prayer and the revelation of God's grace, the headaches were gone; and his strength was renewed. We felt joy again as we listened to grace teaching every morning. Things began to happen that we had been waiting for.

Happiness overflowed as we stood in a circle together with the staff of our new church. We had only been open a few years, but we had been able to grow into a new building. Though the numbers of people were good, we didn't realize that some things were unwell with the members of our new church. Growth in a church cannot be measured only by the number of people attending. We needed to make sure that new people were accepting the gospel of salvation, that those new believers were also growing, and that our vision was truly being multiplied. At times, in the culture of Brazil, people seemed to be with you by the outward actions; but their heart was elsewhere.

"Your life and your thoughts are made new everyday by the Word of God!" Paul preached with enthusiasm.

However, Paul and I were oblivious to what was coming. The church building with expensive rent had two floors—the top floor was where we held our services, and the bottom was a secondhand clothing store that helped to pay for the rent. The building was organized to be used every day with English and crochet classes, women's tea parties, a country fair, and big Christmas events. We had everything to look forward to; and we believed that the church, a community of like-minded people, had a bright future. Unfortunately, there was an unseen bump in the road ahead for us.

At the back of the church stood some grumblers, arms folded and whispering to each other. Not long after, our small church experienced its first split.

Criticism can be helpful if it is open, but behind our backs to everyone in the church other than us was harmful. They had another agenda in mind; and it had nothing to do with the well-being of our church. They eventually left but not before influencing the rest of the members. In fact, the majority of our church was invited to try out the newer church across town in Holambra. It is common among the Brazilian Christians to visit other churches, and it can be just as innocent as visiting friends in their living rooms. I had to learn to trust God with the people that he gave us, and to be happy for the members wherever they went, even if it wasn't at our church. The ones who stayed and tried to make things better, I learned to recognize them as gold.

During that painful time, we learned that grace was evident when the church was full, and grace was there when the church was almost empty. God was still the same.

"Enjoy the small numbers!" a Dutchman had told us when we were at the beginning of the church plant.

My friend Cody encouraged me to let the people go who were not growing and thriving. She said that those people were a like a weight holding down a balloon that was meant to fly upward.

Through time, I understood. Filling up a church was not only about numbers. It was all about making disciples and training leaders. Looking around the room, there was a varied group of people; and some didn't even like one another! To top it off, we were a Dutch-American couple. We had a way to go before we could reach new people, let alone work together as a team. It would take time, patience, and pruning; but eventually, we would get there.

I was always tempted to go after the ones who left, but Paul always assured me that the ones who were meant to stay with us would stay. Many church-goers were invited to leave with the other small group of grumblers. In the end, a few left; but the rest were unmovable and stayed with us and our vision.

"I don't want to force anyone to stay," Paul said. "Let them be happy and follow Jesus wherever they choose to go."

It was the best way to let go of a painful situation that was out of our hands; but with fewer people, the tithing went down. Still, we were able to pay a lot of the rent out of our own pockets. It was our dream, and it wasn't over yet. It was only the beginning!

During the beginning of our church plant, we also experienced an increase in spiritual warfare. In the year ahead, we were tested like never before. Our home was broken into, our car was stolen, and there were difficulties with family living overseas. It had been a very painful year; but as it ended and God gave victory after victory, our enthusiasm was bright without a shadow cast upon it.

Our Wednesday night services were filled as many came from negative church experiences to hear more about Jesus and His grace. Paul taught from a small handbook that was written by a man from the Netherlands. It captured Scriptures about healing, a new identity, prayer, and prosperity, which was, in essence, "being blessed in order to be a blessing." However, when we finished our study of the handbook, the number of people kept dwindling. I was given the Wednesday night slot, and I intended to reach the women of our church with a theme about wisdom in daily life.

One Wednesday evening, we had our Bible study in the book of Proverbs. We used a study guide by Pastor John van Harn. As it was a small group, we decided to form a circle of chairs downstairs, where the secondhand store was located. Lightweight tablecloths were thrown neatly over the racks of colorful dresses, and a table was there with a selection of used toys. The glass door was left open in the front; and a bright light was on, attracting bugs. Maybe a latecomer could come right in if need be.

I opened the Bible to Proverbs; and after prayer, we began to discuss the benefits of wisdom. The front door slid open, and a thin person with a hoodie that partially covered the face slinked in to where we were sitting. Most of the group were women; but Henrique, our foster Brazilian son, was there.

My head snapped to the side to see who was coming in, and one of the women began to shake after the stranger entered under an ominous cloud.

"I need money, and I heard that there is a lot of it rolling over here!"

Our Bible study group stayed still like ice. The puzzled look on our faces portrayed the lack of comprehension of what exactly was going on.

"Just a joke!" he said as he removed his hoodie and revealed that he was a young man who had visited before and even played the saxophone in the worship service. He lived at a halfway house in town that helped men recovering from addictions. He was so young and thin, and he even looked hungry. Was it really a joke, or had he lost his nerve when he saw that we had open Bibles on our laps?

"Can I pray for you?" I asked without even thinking or answering him.

It was like I was in a fog that would quickly pass. I needed to share the hope of the gospel, and the risk I took was unimportant at the time. I didn't have time to consider the consequences or what could happen next.

"Please pray for me! I need help, and I have struggled with addictions for a long time," he said as he opened his wounded heart to us all.

We gathered around the young man, and he closed his eyes to quietly receive the prayer.

Afterward, he said softly, "You are all golden." He looked around the group. "When I look at you with my spiritual eyes, I see you as golden."

Someone from our Bible study group laughed a shaky sigh of relief; then the visitor quietly walked out of the building without another word.

"I was so scared!" Kaira said.

"Me, too," said Lilla.

Henrique shook his head but didn't say a word. He knew the young man and would try to help him if he could.

"What made you think to pray?" asked Josi. "Do you think that he was really joking, or did he change his mind about robbing us?"

"I didn't think about it at all," I said. "It must have been the Lord helping me because all that I wanted to do was pray for him."

We talked a little more before we finished the Bible study. A man had come in to rob us; but instead, he found real gold. The next week, the Wednesday night Bible study was full of several of the men who hadn't been coming on a regular basis. Each one looked out for their neighbor, and we were all safe—protected from danger and the fear of danger by the Lord. Not another word was shared about the young man who came by, and we never heard of him again after that evening.

CHAPTER 37

# A Tropical Storm

*"Life isn't about waiting for the storm to pass.
It's about learning to dance in the rain."*[21]

—Vivian Greene

## Ilhabela

March 2019

With each passing day, more children were added to the shelter at Lar Feliz Ilhabela. Often, whole families came with their siblings because one or both parents were drug-users. There were also complicated cases involving troubled teens who came to live there. When the teens arrived at the children's home, they were like hurricanes in human form. More often than not, they left their homes behind with destruction in their wake. Some had committed crimes that were not punished.

One teen, Roberto, was causing much trouble for Petra and Veronica; so, Veronica suggested they try to get to know him and his background in order to better understand his behavior.

It was usually true that behind the life of a rebellious boy was a sad tale of rejection. It began with one or both of his parents, then his schoolteachers,

---

21 Viviane Greene, *Good Mourning: What Death Teaches Us About Life* (Los Angeles, Times Mirror Company, January 1, 1992).

and ultimately ended with the rejection of society. In many families, it was something that continued to repeat itself like a circle of doom. One generation presented itself in the worst way to the next, and so the pattern continued. Only hope in God and a series of miracles would ever change it. It also took an indefinite amount of time and patience.

Living in the heat of violent arguments and dealing with runaway teens at times brought an end to the patience of the most productive of staff. It would be nice to find a quick answer when there wasn't one.

Some of these teens came to us under the PPCAM program. This was an organization that helped place violent, rebellious teens—whose lives were threatened by fellow gang members—in children's shelters, where they were completely unknown and, for the most part, hidden away.

"Don't take her picture! It's not allowed!" Paul whispered in my ear as I took pictures of the children doing arts and crafts around the table. I understood; but sadly, I deleted the picture of the beautiful girl with a wide-open smile holding her homemade greeting card that she had painted. I thought about all the pictures that I had of our own kids and the babies that I had worked with in the past. Taking pictures was a way of capturing memories for me, but it was a life-threatening situation for someone else.

Michael was a tall and strong young man, who had been sent to the home in Jaguariúna. It started off so promising; but he began to be bored of the country life, and he started running away and stealing things.

Steven was an intelligent boy, living at Ilhabela, who was learning to speak English rapidly. He was easy to talk to, friendly, and cooperative. His parents, who were ministers at the Assembly of God church, had both passed away, leaving him and his only sister. He had carved out a place in our hearts as we spent time talking with him.

As a former gang member, his life was always at risk; and he was constantly looking over his shoulder. He began skipping school and even missing the English class that he loved without giving any good reason.

While I was doing crafts, and waiting on Paul to finish with his endless meetings, I heard Petra struggling with one of the boys.

Petra took a firm hand. "You must get up and go to school!"

"You can't make me!" Steven said with his nose pressed nearly to Petra's.

"You have to think about your future!" Petra said.

It was clear that Petra was under a great deal of stress, and she began to develop this unusual itching sensation in her lower arms. Her skin was pink with irritation.

"I don't know what to do with him," Petra later confided in us.

It was later decided by the judge's technical team of social workers and psychologists that for his own safety, Steven would be moved to the Lar Feliz in Jaguariúna. When he arrived, he gave a friendly wave to me while I was at the baby house; and he met several men workers. Finally, he had found some Christian men that he could really talk to. My heart soared with hope that this young man finally had a chance to live up to his potential. Everything was new and different. At first, it was a welcome change, but he lasted only a month; and then he was moved to a city far away that no one knew about.

"It's close to Sao Paulo," someone said.

There were a whole lot of places including suburbs that were near that monstrous big city. He could be just about anywhere.

Veronica wanted to know how he was doing and asked someone who had been in charge.

"He's good," said the official.

It was all the news that we would ever hear about Steven; but at least, we knew that he was good.

One evening, while we were having dinner, Paul received text after text from Petra. He called to find out more. It was really the worst situation that I had ever heard of at that point, and it made the skin on the back of my neck crawl.

"Oh, I don't know what to do! How can they do this?"

"Slow down, and tell me what happened," Paul said in Dutch.

"We are being sent a new teenage boy who was charged with raping a minor! They are sending him to our home because they fear that he will be murdered in prison."

"So, they are sending him to a children's home, where at least six minor girls are living?" Paul asked in disbelief.

"They could be in danger!"

"We must stop this! Call a meeting with the judge."

The very next day, the new boy was placed in the children's home with the little girls, boys, and babies. It was against the protocol of Lar Feliz. Petra and Veronica traveled to the judge's office the next week. The judge was a young man with cold eyes that didn't quite light up when he smiled. The judge's decision was final, and we heard later that evening.

Petra and Veronica appeared in front of the small desk in his office. They brought the case of the teen boy who had raped, hoping for a different outcome; but they were greatly disappointed.

The judge had already made his final decision before talking to Petra and Veronica. His reasoning was that Ilhabela is rich and has the means to take care of the boy. And because the judge wanted the boy off the streets—he would stay!

The beautiful island of Ilhabela had a lot of hidden problems. There were so many young people who were using drugs, combined with poverty here, there, and everywhere. The judge was tired and just wanted to go home at a decent hour that night. There was not a thing that any of us could do.

There had been little respect for their professional input. A final decision was made, and there was no use fighting it. In the coming days, they would have to make it work.

The children's court was left between a rock and a hard place. They had to consider the safety of the other children in a shelter, but what could they do with a rebellious teenage boy who had committed a crime and needed help? Should he be placed in a situation where his life light would quickly be snuffed out? Or should he be given one last chance? Everyone deserves one last chance to learn from their mistakes and do better. At least, that is what the Brazilian officials mostly thought in the area where black and white is mixed into gray.

Veronica invited Petra to go to the home group of her church. Though she was tired after a twelve-hour working day and the emotional weight of the teen boy's situation rested heavily on her, Petra agreed to go. It was there that she first met Franklin and got to know him better during Bible study and prayer.

It was a six-hour drive to Ilhabela from Holambra, and we listened to praise and worship music the whole way there. We speedily arrived at the line for the ferry ahead of schedule. The still sea water meant that we could drive onto the large boat without any wait. Once on the island, we checked into our rooms at the friendly but cheap hotel with no frills and cold cement floors. We changed clothes and prepared to go visit the children at the home. Later, we would go out for dinner to discuss a plan of action.

Once arriving at the home, we saw the troubled figure of Petra.

"The two teen boys have run away! I've tried, but I can't find them; and I call, but they don't answer."

"We will use the time to visit the other children then," Paul said over his shoulder as he hurriedly walked into the home. I tried to keep up while carrying tote bags full of art supplies. We were greeted by some small, friendly golden-brown faces. There were hugs all around as the children greeted us coming in.

In the evening, we talked together with Veronica and Petra. I didn't have much advice to give, and I came along to do what I was good at. I came to only listen.

In the midst of the spiritual storm with the difficult teenagers, it started to become clear to Paul that even though he wanted to keep going with the home, it was almost impossible because of the distance. He needed to have his "hands in the dough," as they say in Brazil.

CHAPTER 38
# A Day at the Big Tent

*"They that sow in tears shall reap in joy. He that goeth forth and weepeth, bearing precious seed, shall doubtless come again with rejoicing, bringing his sheaves with him."*

Psalm 126:5-6

## Jaguariúna
### 2019

"Let's join the circus," Rodrigo the psychologist said. He led the way to the micro-bus, along with myself, some other monitors, and many teens dressed in their workout clothing.

Once on the bus, we traveled to Mogi Mirim, where a new program was being presented. We were shown a new facility that included a library, an eating lounge, and a gym with a tightrope. To our amazement, there were circus workers there who were training anyone who wanted to climb up. It seemed risky, but the adrenaline rush would help keep children who were coming after school out of trouble and off the streets.

"What have we learned?" A young man jumped off the trapeze, his eyes exploring the crowd of children.

"I have learned, through this experience, to permit myself to connect with my inner child. This resource is significant for us to utilize in our experiences. A child is pure and innocent and can forgive and resolve situations of conflict in a healthy way," said Cris, another psychologist from Lar Feliz. "I would like to share with you my new desire that all the children here will never withdraw from their inner child."

It was a very profound statement that said it all for me. The after-school program was a plan B to consider if our children's home swindled and closed. A new trend in Brazil, this program was a method in helping needy families with mothers who were working. Rather than take the children completely out of the home, they would be taken care of during the day and even educated until they could return home in the evenings. Many times, the children returned to single parent families who never knew a father figure.

What a wonderful day it had been—a memory that would stay in my heart forever. As we rode the bus back to Lar Feliz, I thought about my whole time working at the children's shelter. My passion had been loving and helping the children. They were my reason for everything I did. Even after they moved away, I was able to keep in touch with some who had been adopted into new families. The moments I got to spend with them, watching them grow, were golden to me.

CHAPTER 39

# Life in the Jungle

*"This saith the LORD; 'Cursed be the man that trusteth in man, and maketh flesh his arm, and whose heart departeth from the LORD. For he shall be like the heath in the desert, and shall not see when good cometh; but shall inhabit the parched places in the wilderness, in a salt land and not inhabited.'"*

Jeremiah 17:5-6

We traveled by car during the dark night to a neighborhood just off the highway once we reached Mogi Mirim. It was called "the Jungle," but there was nothing green living in it—only sad, desperate people. As we cautiously pulled along the narrow street with cookie-cutter, cement-colored government houses, we came to a familiar home and pulled to a stop. All along the street were children, some playing with soccer balls while others were laughing at a joke, hands cupped over their mouths. The sweet, sickly smell of smoke penetrated the air as we got out of the car.

Once we entered the home where a church was meeting, we were greeted with warm hugs, smiles, and small cups of sweet, yet strong, Brazilian coffee made the old-fashioned way without an espresso machine. The weather was very humid, and the people there were modestly dressed in shorts and sandals. No one there possessed a Bible, and they barely possessed enough food to get through the week.

The law in the neighborhood was not in the hands of the police, but it was in the hands of a few young and powerful lords with guns. Many women and children lived abandoned but certainly not needful of anyone's pity. Their husbands were away, sometimes for months, in prison. The brave women would venture out a few times a week to hear the Word of the Lord and learn about grace. They shared what little they had with those in need. One woman named Daiane had a wide smile and a thick hug; and she was at the little home church whenever the doors were opened.

"Thank you, Jesus, for giving me life," she said often. She brought what things she could to help others; she taught children about Jesus; and most importantly, she was always faithful in attending church. She was often the first one there and the last to leave. She lived in primitive conditions, and she didn't have much income to take care of her young daughters, but she was spiritually wealthy and filled with unstoppable joy.

I walked toward the back of the veranda and encountered someone there with a piece of chocolate cake.

"Do you want some, Honey?" she asked with a few teeth missing from her grin.

Whenever a Brazilian was eating a snack, they always offered something. They just don't feel comfortable eating while someone else might be hungry. I had already been offered half a banana, half a candy bar, and half a sandwich at one time or another. The poor were always so kind. They had little, but they always tried to share what they did have.

"It's time for the service to start." Pastor Paul's voice was heard above the rumble of conversations around the coffee and the chocolate cake.

The singer came forward and called the people to worship. "Let those who are able, stand; and let's start with prayer."

Half of the congregation rose and began to clap to the tempo of the music. After three songs, the pastor gave a short but powerful message about grace and salvation through Jesus. He offered hope with the last verse that he shared. It ended in a beautiful way; some came to the front and reached out for prayer, while others stayed seated. Every chair that was set up that night was filled with a body who needed the encouragement of the Word and the unending hope and comfort of the Holy Spirit.

Paul and I got into our car to return home. It had been a pleasant evening. We could have easily gone out for dinner or stayed home and rested; but the brightened faces of the people and the tired hands now lifted were well worth the time that it took to go to the Jungle that Saturday night.

## CHAPTER 40
## *Amor*

*"Let him kiss me with the kisses of his mouth: for thy love is better than wine."*

Song of Songs 1:2

# Ilhabela
## 2020

While the children's home at Ilhabela had been facing many difficulties, a bright light was shining; and that light was a local church. The pastor's wife, who was the shepherd over the women and teenage girls, took Petra and Veronica under her wings; and they began to rest in the joy of knowing what God had for the future was better than anything that they could imagine. The pastor and his wife believed that Jesus was everything that we could want or need, and they believed that God wanted to make a change in Brazil. The church courageously reached out to teen girls in the schools and on the streets with the good news of the gospel. God had a better way and life for them! They reached out to the youth with addiction problems and the occasional wanderer passing through.

The church, located by the sea, was filled with youth in sandy *chinelo*, tourists with designer bags, and everything in between. The Holy Spirit filled that beautiful, old building, and the gospel gloriously went forth every week in that place.

The first time that we saw Franklin, it was a brief encounter when we visited Petra's church by the sea. He brushed past her quickly as she took her seat. She was beautiful in a white pants outfit that complemented her slim waist. He disappeared, and we didn't get a chance to introduce ourselves.

They had decided not to date right away, so Petra's heart had to be lassoed in because it was her desire to have a steady relationship.

Franklin later asked if she would be willing to text back and forth. Petra agreed, deciding that this arrangement sounded better than nothing. Besides, she really could use a friend to talk to. They got to know each other more personally through texting back and forth.

She began to tell Franklin all about her day and then about her frustrations at work; she talked about the Bible study that was held the week before; and finally, she told him about her dreams for the future and how she wanted to reach out to pregnant teenage girls.

Franklin texted her about his family, his childhood, and his move from northern Brazil to Ilhabela, where his heart had found a home. He told about his challenging job of working with a young autistic boy during school. He also had dreams and plans—like studying to be a federal policeman. He had a bright future in mind.

Thus began their written relationship. They were closer, even though they were apart.

The next morning, Petra received terrible news through a phone call. Missionaries living far away from their homeland received all bad news that way.

She learned that her mother had passed away after suffering from chronic illness.

Petra booked the flight and spent the time with her family—grieving and living. They looked at pictures and shared memories of the good days when her mother was strong and happy. Now she was with Jesus.

While she was at home with her family, Petra made a decision. The pace was slow and relaxing, and she remembered her dreams that had been pushed aside during her work at the children's home. She did some soul-searching on the plane trip back to Brazil.

"We need to have a meeting and talk in person," Petra said to Paul. "Have Jill be there, too!"

Paul and I were halfway to the island when we got the message. We would meet with Petra that very evening at a Syrian pizza restaurant by the beach.

"I have some news, and you are not going to like it at all," Petra said shyly.

"Well, go on," said Paul.

"I'm leaving my work at Lar Feliz," said Petra.

I didn't quite know how to respond and hid my disappointment with a thin smile.

"Petra, we want you to be happy. You need to pursue your God-given dreams."

"We will just have to look for your replacement. Maybe there is someone on the island who would do it," said Paul.

Petra nodded woodenly.

## CHAPTER 41
## Change of Plans

*"For I know the thoughts that I think toward you,' saith the LORD, 'thoughts of peace, and not of evil, to give you an expected end."*

Jeremiah 29:11

### Holambra
January 2020

Pastor Rodolfo, a pastor from Mogi Mirim, shared the verse from Jeremiah at the church. It was Vision Sunday, and we anxiously looked to the Lord for guidance of what He was saying for the year.

"Surely, the year 2020 will be filled with vision and all kinds of good happenings," I told Paul later that evening.

Our year was meticulously planned from January until October when we had planned to visit the Netherlands. In January, we would hand out Bibles to every home in Holambra, partnering with different churches and with young volunteers from Youth With a Mission. Also, a team from Georgia would come for three months to hold small group conversations about the gospel of grace. I almost already felt tired thinking about all our plans and goals for 2020!

The annual women's tea was underway. I was organizing a testimony, the decorations, the color scheme, the food, and who to invite from what village.

I would organize the main sermon because God had laid it on my heart. "He is more than enough," would be the message.

The women of the church, who were mainly living in Holambra, buzzed like honeybees, transforming the long, colorless sanctuary into a forest of bright yellow flowers and peaceful palms. The decorations were made with such love in the hopes that each woman would feel loved and at home. It seemed to be working as the women started to arrive with eagerness. To mark the special day, many wanted their pictures taken with me as the event speaker, as well as with their family members. A van load arrived from the town of Mogi Mirim; and Daiane came out all smiles, passing out warm Jesus hugs to everyone who crossed her path.

The potluck dessert table with coffee and juice had more to offer than any single restaurant buffet. Each beautiful plate was filled with divine delicacies like coconut cream pie, fish salad sandwiches, and chocolate cookies. The volunteers' mouths were starting to water. I assured the men who came to help in the kitchen that they could enjoy the leftovers once the luncheon was finished. There was plenty of food, and there would be more than enough left over. The women would have their service upstairs, and the men would have their afternoon snack in peace. It was a perfect exchange, and many men came to help.

Once the tea was nearly over, I went upstairs to the sanctuary to grab a few quiet minutes and prepare my heart when suddenly, my phone pinged. A message from my friend, Debora, came in.

"Ola!" her message began.

Debora went on to explain a news report that they had recently watched about a virus spreading throughout China. "My family heard that the world is coming to an end this April. Is it true? Do you know when Jesus is coming back?"

I had heard about the virus. I was hoping against hope that it wouldn't hit Brazil as badly as it had in China.

I thoughtfully answered Debora's question. "No, Debora. We don't know the day, the hour, or the month that Jesus is coming back. It is a mystery, and we need to be ready at any time. I will come by later, and we can talk. Hopefully, this virus won't come to Brazil, but we should be careful and do everything we can to prevent it." I clicked "Send" and then stood up to begin the women's service.

After the last amen, it was evident that a joy-filled service had taken place and the Holy Spirit had moved in hearts. Smiles were recorded as the last few photos were taken on cell phones. The kitchen was wiped down; the lights were turned off; and the ladies went home with full hearts.

CHAPTER 42

# The Beginning of the End

*"When thou passest through the waters, I will be with thee; and through the rivers, they shall not overflow thee: when thou walkest through the fire, thou shalt not be burned; neither shall the flame kindle upon thee."*

Isaiah 43:2

## Ilhabela
February 2020

Franklin finally had a revelation, and he eagerly desired to share it with his friend, Petra. He had peace, and he wanted to start dating her!

Petra, after getting to know Franklin a little better, really wanted to start dating, too.

## Holambra
April 2020

The wave of Covid-19 had reached the state of Sao Paulo. The faith rose in the church leadership in the nation, and they indicated to the people that Covid-19 would not come near. It was the European flu, after all; and Brazilians had nothing to fear.

I held on to my new Bible as I read Psalm 91:1 again and again: *"He that dwelleth in the secret place of the Most High shall abide under the shadow of the Almighty."*

Clouds of uneasiness settled as I read and meditated on the truths of that Psalm—a Psalm that was practically memorized in Brazil and printed on everything from tea towels to cards. Many Bibles were left open in homes at precisely Psalm 91. It wasn't only for my life that I worried. My heart lived in several locations. I was afraid for my family in Ohio, and now I couldn't easily travel if something would happen.

Our children, Isa and Jeremy, were living in the state of Texas; and Paul's family was in the Netherlands. My heart was stretched and broken, existing in several different places on the globe. I realized at that time that I was better off not watching the daily news, but I spent my extra time meditating on the Word of God, which brought me peace.

My heart burned for Brazil, a developing land with the innocence of a trusting child looking for truth in all the wrong places. The cases increased, growing steadily worse until the death toll began to climb and spread closer to our town; closer to our church; and closer to Lar Feliz, the children's home.

"Daiane is sick! The church needs to pray!"

It was sent around the church group chat about the seriousness of her case as a thirty-six-year-old woman with two young daughters.

The church continued to pray as more members began to contract the virus. Bene and Sidnei, a faithful couple from the church, were also home sick from the virus.

"Services are canceled!"

A bulletin was placed on the church Facebook page: "We will be having services online until further notice."

Daiane from Mogi Mirim continued to grow worse as she was put on a ventilator in the ICU ward. We had to keep praying! Though some churches felt the faith to keep meeting in public, Pastor Paul decided against it. Meeting together would only increase the spread of the virus. We had to protect the members from the infectious spread.

"The church is not a building. The church is us: a living, breathing organism. We are a church in movement. We are not contained in just the four walls of our building."

Paul ended his message with this challenge. Everywhere around, people were hungry and hurting. Many were sick and dying.

This challenge was laid before us. This was to be the church's shining hour. A big decision would be made as to the large building we had been renting. Without a weekly offering, it would be very difficult to pay the high rent. We would trust God and let go. The decision seemed to be made for us when a lockdown was instituted in the state of Sao Paulo in Brazil. No one would be or should be going to the traditional Sunday evening service in our part of the land. It was time for us to move; and just as the stakes of a big tent were picked up to relocate, we began to put the life of the church into cardboard boxes, leaving behind the bare white walls. We would have to follow the cloud of glory wherever it took us.

## Holambra
### In lockdown

"Mom, I won't be able to fly home for your birthday this year. There is a travel ban, and we are strongly discouraged from traveling to other countries," I said.

"That's okay. We can see each other when we video chat," my mom reassured me.

The virus was multiplying rapidly in the States, and it was just as quickly multiplying in Brazil. It was impossible for Paul and me to travel to see our loved ones. Our plans, which had included a reunion with our missionary school, were completely wiped off the table. Instead of planning for the year, we had to take each week as it was. We spent lots of time in the garden, and we went for walks and studied the Word of God.

It was monotonous, at times, for me; and Paul began to complain about not being able to go out to restaurants. Every day, we played games and talked with each other. All our recreational and social options had changed. The shopping malls were closed, and church services were held online. We quickly learned how to make encouraging videos with the help of Henrique and Kaira, and we held children's services online with Josi using some puppets.

Everything had suddenly changed. Would anything be the same as before? I felt a heavy sense of discouragement at times, and I even felt trapped in a way. During my whole missionary career, I had always found a way to make it back home to Ohio for visits. Now, all six of my elderly aunts and my mother were at risk of catching the virus, and I must stay in Brazil at home. The Lord's presence comforted me during those times; and I had to continually set my thoughts toward Jesus, or the anxiety and fear would overtake me until I found it hard to sleep at night.

I received a voice text from my friend, Cody, from the Netherlands.

"Jill, how are you doing there? I watched some things on the news," she wrote.

We chatted back and forth about our different situations, and she assured me that Daiane would be in their prayers.

She then proceeded to asked if I would be interested in partnering with Redemption Church in the Netherlands on a project called Gracious Daughters—a social media outreach for women only. She wanted me to use my Portuguese to head up the Brazilian page.

Now, I am not normally an office person. I was pretty much left behind in computer skills, and my Portuguese was at a level of talking with children because I had been working with only children for over ten years. "I will do it! Sounds great!" I heard myself say to Cody.

"You don't know anything about the computer!" Paul stated the obvious to me after I hung up.

"All things are possible with God.[22] Where there is a will, there is a way," I told myself, and I was anxious to learn.

---

[22] Matthew 19:26

CHAPTER 43

# Light in Their Dwellings

*"They saw not one another, neither rose any from his place for three days: but all the children of Israel had light in their dwellings."*

Exodus 10:23

Pastor Joshua McCauley closed his devotional for Monday morning with a call to the Lord's supper, or communion. I put aside my notebook. Notes were taken that I would later translate and put into the church community group. Paul and I ate the bread and drank the grape juice, remembering the wonderful sacrifice of Jesus our Savior.

Paul then looked at his phone and read the message, "Daiane might come off the ventilator today. Praise the Lord!"

While it was still morning light, we decided to go for a long walk together. Being in quarantine, we weren't supposed to go out around other people. Paul would still work once a day at Lar Feliz, but I was often isolated at home.

We put on our masks and protective hats; and we ventured out past the calm, serene lake to the roof-covered park before making a turn to go up a steep hill to the center of town. Paul always walked in front, and I took slow, dragging steps just behind him. The sun was already hot and beating down on the street, which had the fragrance of burnt flesh from the chicken factory nearby. Just a little further over the hill, we would reach shade and a lake that always had a nice breeze with gardens, animals, and luscious tall trees.

*Just a little farther! You can make it!*

Paul quickly made it to the top with only a little effort, but I felt like I would die. I was breathless and beet red when we finally made it to the second-hand clothing store at the top of the hill.

"Do you need some water?" Lilla, the manager, asked.

"Sure, but we need to keep going."

We walked for over an hour, enjoying breathtaking views of rural Holambra; we walked to the windmill at the entrance of town, passing beautiful gardens and lovely shade trees. It had been a picturesque morning, and we finally returned home for a tall glass of bubbling mineral water with a slice of lime.

Later that evening, we received the bad news that Daiane had lost her battle against COVID—a young woman in the prime of her life. My heart sank to my ankles as I thought of her two young girls now orphaned. All around, we were hearing death notices of friends and acquaintances. It seemed that everyone in Brazil had lost someone they loved. The spirit of grief was flowing from home to home.

# Ilhabela
## April 2020

"We are in lock down, and it is not going well!" Petra texted us as it continued to rain steadily at Ilhabela. She gave us daily updates of how it was going on the island.

"The new boy is causing so much trouble; you wouldn't believe it. No one can come to the island, and no one can leave the island. The cases of COVID are increasing by the day."

"Tell the judge that we want to have a virtual meeting this week, and I will be there," Paul answered

"Good!"

Petra still continued to text Franklin, until one day he made a decision.

He wanted to start dating, but it was quarantine. No one was allowed out because of the lockdown. So, Petra told Franklin that he would have to wait! Petra in her training was always following the rules.

After talking it over at length, Petra agreed that they could see each other a few times during the lockdown if they were careful and used their masks. Franklin was elated!

Petra was a strong warrior, who was ready to stand her ground. It was not often that things fell together so quickly and easily. This new relationship with Franklin did seem to be just that. It was easy and beautiful, like a sunny Sunday afternoon when everything seemed just right with the world.

Franklin came by so that they could pray. They bowed their heads and remembered all the present needs. It had been one calamity after another this year; but in the cocoon of their togetherness, every storm was calm and as it should be.

## Lar Feliz, Jaguariúna
May 2020

The staff gathered around the table at the dining room one day eating crispy fried chicken, garlic rice, and creamy beans with a lettuce and tomato salad.

Earlier that week, Paul's virtual meeting with the judge and technical staff of Ilhabela had gone sour. Paul told the staff that during the meeting, the judge appeared to be disconnected—like a door was slammed in his face. Without giving any credit to their opinions and feelings, the judge then decided to let the teenage boy who was a threat to the rest of the children stay at the home. The reason was given that the council of Ilhabela was wealthy. They had the means and a beautiful home where a needy teenage boy could stay. It was disappointing and without a concrete solution. They held the lives of the other children in their hands and not only the poor teenage boy's.

"We will have to give up the home at Ilhabela. It's just not possible to run it like it should be run if we are unable to get there. Those boys are causing all kinds of trouble, and I have no way of solving it when I am far away," said Pastor Paul.

"There are some things that a phone call doesn't solve, and being far away is an issue that is insurmountable. We are at an impasse," said Solange the psychologist.

"Also, on another subject, Jill said something to me this morning that really got me thinking. Is Pastor Junior going ahead with the church plant on our property? Or has it been delegated to someone else?"

Smack dab in the middle of the two farms owned by Lar Feliz was a little country church that had been built recently by the Four-Square denomination of Brazil under the guidance of Pastor Junior, who had a heart for the rural neighborhood surrounding Lar Feliz. It was a small building that was nestled in the colorful Brazilian countryside, where toucans were spotted occasionally, along with parrots and other wildlife.

The neighborhood there included ranchers who owned beautiful Arabian horses, the sugarcane fields across the way, and skinny cows who ate the grass underneath the mango trees. There were not many people who were seen during daylight hours, and there were some second homes of individuals who traveled from the city of Sao Paulo. The neighborhood illuminated peace during the daylight hours; and at night, the darkness hid the many families who were living behind the main dirt road. It was rustic living, not unlike the cowboys who worked hard on the farm all day in short leather boots, cut-up jeans, and hats. They were different than the town people who went out to the restaurants for lunch with French manicures and freshly cut hair donning their high heels. The country people worked hard; and it showed in their faces, in their open friendliness, and in their to-the-point manner.

The country church that was built on Lar Feliz land had only a handful of regular members—about thirty—all from only a couple families. The vision that Pastor Junior had was not the same as Pastora Debora's, the woman pastor who took over the church in town. It was not for her, and she had no idea how she would find the time to pastor a second church in the rural area away from town.

Paul called Pastora Debora to see how things were going for her with the church building that was located on our land. He told me later that he had the idea that the Four-Square Church was ready to give up their building located in the rural area.

Pastora Debora suggested that we hold a meeting with their pastors and lawyers present. A week later, a small group arrived at our home. Pastora Debora carried a beautifully potted yellow orchid in a glass bowl, which she handed to me with kindness. Her bright smile was hidden behind a medical mask; and no one greeted one another with a handshake or a hug, as was custom in Brazil. Nothing was business as usual.

As we sat in a circle on the back veranda, we opened in prayer.

"Lord, we come to you today because we need to hear Your voice and be guided by You in Your wisdom and perfect will.'

"Amen," several voices chimed as bowed heads were lifted.

"As we all know," Paul began, "the arrangement of the church on our land has not really worked out as we hoped.

A deal had been made with the Four-Square Church: the use of the land on Lar Feliz property in exchange for some legal work that would put the title deed right.

The young woman lawyer from the church nodded and said, "We are at an impasse. The only thing further is to return the land back to Lar Feliz."

"Before we decide, I need to ask Pastora Debora something," I said quietly as all the eyes of the group turned in my direction. "What is your vision for this building? If God gave you a vision for it, maybe it is better not to give up just yet."

Pastor Debora took a swallow of water as she answered, "This building is not my vision. I want to reach the people in town. This is a rural neighborhood far out from where I have any contact. It would be great if your church could take over this work. I am in complete agreement with the idea."

Paul laid his offer on the table. "We will pay for all the construction work on the church building to be paid off in a year's time or sooner if the Lord provides."

"You have a deal!" Pastor Junior said as he rejoicingly jumped to his feet. It was unanimous.

It was a moment of prosperity during a dark famine when all expectations were bleak. It was a moment of friendship and help when any competition between churches dwindled to nothing—the contrast of joy when recently there was nothing to be happy about, new life when death was all around.

"I guess we are moving," Paul said later that evening. "I'm glad that I listened to you!"

As we warmly embraced, I said, "Too bad that doesn't happen more often," and we laughed together.

## CHAPTER 44
# *Almost Home*

*"They which builded on the wall, and they that bare burdens, with those that laded, every one with one of his hands wrought in the work, and with the other hand held a weapon."*

Nehemiah 4:17

### Lar Feliz, Jaguariúna
2005

I walked out into the open field catty-corner to the little boys' home, holding a small child on my hip. Rosalee, a missionary, and another male monitor and I were with a group of children about to pray.

"Lord, You know that we need land to build a permanent home for Lar Feliz and the children. This land we dedicate to you, Lord Jesus," Rosalee prayed.

At that moment, we all raised our hands to the sky and prayed together out loud. It was with faith like children that the little ones, as well as the adults, prayed and dedicated that very spot on the land, which at the time was only an open field with dry prickly grass. This land, blessed by the Lord, would one day be the place of a new and growing church, *Comunidade Novo e Livre*. This new place would also hold a community center, where visions from different churches were joined together under God and His grace.

## Lar Feliz Community Center
2020

In the narrow space that would serve as the sanctuary of the new location of CNL, Sidnei was hard at work, installing the lights and taking care of every detail.

While he worked, he prayed, "Lord, let this be a house of prayer. Let this be a place where young people will come to know you. Amen!"

Henrique was building the sound equipment, something that came completely natural to him, though he had only on-the-job training. He was a gifted musician with a good ear.

Luis, the husband of the secretary, Sonia, worked faithfully cleaning the tiled floors and watering the plants. He had a new life in Jesus since coming to our new church location. Whenever the doors were opened, he was there cleaning, making coffee, or listening to the Word of God.

A loud crackle and bang filled the air with bright fireworks for the New Year as a celebration took place—the year 2020 was finally over.

Johan and Brenda, a couple from the Netherlands, joined in with a Dutch team, as well as Isa, our daughter who had traveled from Texas. It was a cautious group, but being out and being together was like finding long-lost friends. Caution was taken without any hugs or handshakes, which was not custom in Brazil; but everyone stayed safe.

"We were not able to come back since March," Johan said.

"That was such a hard time for us then. Glad it is over now. Hopefully, next year will be a better year!" Brenda said to the group cautiously.

"Best year yet!"

Little did we know, it wasn't over yet; but we held out hope that the end was coming soon.

## On the Highway to Ilhabela
March 2021

Paul glided in and out of the line of cars, making great time and arriving earlier than we had planned. We would make it to the ferry before lunch, which meant that we would miss the traffic hours. The women at the home knew how much we liked fresh fish; so they usually fried the catch of the day and served it with warm garlic rice, beans, and salad. This would be our last visit to the island for a long while. The quarantine was finally over; the way was open; and we would go and make our goodbyes to the children's home that we had founded with all the love in our hearts.

Veronica had asked for prayer leading up to the decision. "We are having round-the-clock prayer time every Tuesday. Would you like to join in?"

"Sure thing," I said. "Give me two slots. I'm honestly not ready to give up Ilhabela, but the Lord knows everything. I will be praying that everything will work out according to His plan. He knows what's best for you, for Petra, for the children, and for everyone involved."

A few weeks later, an organization named "Bom Samaritano" was after all the paperwork. They were accepted to be the new boss of the children's home. Paul voiced his relief, but I needed to see with my own eyes that everything was okay.

It was a bright, sunny day when we arrived a little early at the port of Sao Sebastiao where, just across the sea, the ferry would take us to the beautiful island. Lack of wind meant lack of choppiness in the water, and it was a smoother ride. I lathered up my arms and legs with bug repellent, not wanting to leave it to chance of getting another nasty bite from the infamous "Borrachudo," tiny blood-sucking insects that lived only on Ilhabela. We parked on top of the ferry, and a salty breeze blew through our windows as the large boat chugged along. After fifteen minutes and a few photos taken of the aquamarine sea and sky, we arrived on land.

"We are on the way," Paul said in a voice message to Petra.

"Okay, we will be waiting for you at the first house."

The work of Lar Feliz had grown so much that we had to rent a second house across the street where we could fit all the preteen boys. The house was large with big windows and a big shade tree. The first house that was owned by the city council was in a constant state of renovation over the past year. There were typically several workmen hammering, pouring cement, or cutting the grass.

Paul opened the outside door after ringing the bell, and we were greeted by happy, friendly children. Waves and hugs around, we slowly stepped closer to the dining room, where an overused little table filled with food awaited us.

As we prayed and began to eat, the men peeked into the windows, indicating that they were hungry also and ready to eat.

"Tía! I will be so glad when the renovations are finely done. If it isn't the noise, then it is their constant intrusion!" Petra said as she rubbed her arms that were irritated from a rash.

After we ate, we planned. I would do some art projects with the contents of my big, overflowing bag. Paul had organized various meetings with the government officials. Whatever craft I brought to do brought fresh faces of interest and talented hands that could draw and paint whatever the eyes could see. We decided to make greeting cards for all the women who worked at the home. Women's Day was just around the corner, and it was nice for every woman to feel appreciated and inspired.

One thing I knew and often said, "Without God, Lar Feliz wouldn't exist; and without women, Lar Feliz wouldn't exist either!"

"Franklin and I would like to have dinner with you tonight at the *Pimento Cheiro*," said Petra.

"Absolutely, can't wait," I said.

It was a cozy place by the sea, all decorated in red and yellow with fresh herbs planted in pots on the tables. During this visit, I needed to *matar saudade*, a term in Portuguese that meant to kill all your homesickness for a place or a person. It meant, in the practical sense, to see everyone that you wanted to see, eat everywhere that you wanted to eat, and do everything that you wanted to do, knowing that it might be for the last time, at least for a while. I had learned how to adapt to this way of thinking; and together, with Paul, we would do just that!

"We are engaged, and we would like you to translate our wedding ceremony into Dutch," Petra announced to Paul.

"I would love to, and I am honored!" Paul said.

"For sure, we will be there! I would never want to miss it!" I spoke. It was so good that the lock-down days in Brazil seemed to be over!

"Isa will be visiting us. We will even bring her!"

The waves of the ocean gently lapped against the sand not far from our table. The waiters went around from table to table, lighting candles. The sea breeze blew away any anxiety, and there wasn't a bug in sight. The rice was cooked just right; the fresh fish in the cream sauce was salty deliciousness; and the drinks were cold. Just one more day, we would return to our home and work in Holambra and all the business and organizing that it took for running the children's home in Jaguariúna, as well as the church and community center there.

"The Lord knows what He does," I said to Paul as we drove home.

The closing of one chapter meant the opening of the next one.

## CHAPTER 45
# From Death to Life

*"Now unto Him that is able to do exceedingly abundantly above all that we ask or think, according to the power that worketh in us."*

Ephesians 3:20

I was working in my office when I heard something like a cry or a moan.

"Help me! Come here!" said Paul. "There is something terribly wrong with Charlie."

Charlie had been the kindest, wisest animal in our home for nearly twenty years. I raced to the living room to find Charlie with frightened eyes in a continued state of falling on the hard tiled floor. He would try to stand on all fours, only to fall again.

"Maybe he broke a leg." It seemed to be that he had trouble moving his body on one whole side.

"I'll take him to the vet. Hold him!"

Tears mingled with the thick orange coat. "Help me get him in the car!"

Paul drove by himself with Charlie in the back seat. Once at the vet, the tears flowed uncontrollably. It was too soon to say goodbye to such a marvelous dog.

"Charlie had a stroke," Paul said over the phone. "They want us to leave him overnight for observation. There is not much that they can do."

The next morning, we went haltingly to the vet named Renato. "There has been little change," he said.

We walked around to the back, where Charlie was held in an open pen. Charlie's sad eyes told the story that we didn't want to hear. It was time for us to let him go.

"Goodbye, Charlie," I said tenderly through tears as I bent over and hugged him; his thick fur comforted my face one last time. "I will miss you."

I walked to the office, and Paul stayed at his side until the last breath. We left the veterinarian's office hand in hand.

"Let's not get another dog because doing this is just too hard," Paul said as we sat in the car and drove away.

"Deal!"

Along with the death of our dog, there were many deaths around us in our town and among our friends. Everyone had lost a loved one from COVID, and people were literally starving. Many businesses were halted because of lockdown, resulting in people not getting paid, which meant that families were going without necessities to get by. A dark, heavy gloom pervaded the atmosphere around. It was hard to imagine how life had been before.

At Lar Feliz, we continued to receive new children every day. Sometimes, whole families of siblings came, along with new teenage girls who had gotten pregnant. Our home was quickly full again, and we had to hire new workers.

Amid all of this darkness, the women of our church received an invitation to be a light amid this darkness.

"Be awake, daughters! Be ready with lamps during this dark season. God has given you a voice! When we have a revelation of His love and faith the size of a seed of mustard, we will not be afraid or have dread for the future. It's in His hands. In Romans 14:17 it says, 'For the kingdom of God is not meat and drink; but righteousness, and peace, and joy in the Holy Ghost.' Hold onto these things: peace, righteousness, and joy!" Pastor Tara McCauley exhorted during her sermon.[23]

Adriana worked for Lar Feliz for years doing the marketing. Adriana, Paul, and I walked into a neighborhood that was unseen and unknown on the edge of Holambra. There were rows of tiny wooden homes, some with flower gardens, others with toys. We clapped our hands at the door, which was custom in Brazil to let your presence be made known. Doorbells didn't always work, so the clapping gave the sign that a visitor would like to enter.

"Yes?" A mother's head poked out of the door.

Paul stepped forward. "We are here with our church, and we are handing out food baskets. Do you need any help?"

"Yes! We opened our last bit of food, and we didn't know what we were going to do next. My children are hungry, and we have no money because there is no work right now with the flower business."

Sadness filled her tone, and we could see firsthand the desperation of the situation at hand.

Everyone everywhere was struggling, and many had lost someone that they loved. Suddenly, the realization that the church needed to raise more money for food for these helpless people was quite evident. It was a heart-wrenching and unforgettable day for me, and I later cried thinking about it. Would Brazil's economy survive all of this?

"Aunt Pat isn't doing very well. I don't know how long she has. She had been very sick; and now, she's not eating," my mom said on the phone.

"Even though Brazilians are not allowed to travel right now, because I am an American citizen, I can come home to Ohio for a visit," I assured her.

---

23    Tara McCauley, "Daughter With a Voice" (sermon), Gracious Daughters Conference, 2020, Redemption Church, South Africa.

Aunt Pat was a very special person who loved Jesus and God's Word. She was ninety-six years old, but her mind was sharp like a tack. She had gone blind through the years, but her spiritual sight was clearer than ever before. I would be able to visit her one last time in her cozy living room with the lamplight on a soft glow. The peace and the presence of the Lord Jesus was in that small sitting room with a shelf that had pictures of her and her late husband, Vernon, along with books and Bibles. Next to her comfy chair, she had her tape player to listen to her audio books and the occasional gospel music.

She was a woman who had suffered, and she had a gift of listening to people's troubles. When the conversations untangling problems would be stilled, she was often heard to say, "This is true." Afterward, the person went home in peace, having laid down their burdens in that very room.

I had to take the risk of flying home in a pandemic, if only to see her one last time and to say goodbye.

Paul took me to the bus stop in Campinas to travel all the way to Sao Paulo to catch the plane to America. His hug goodbye gave me confidence to make the long journey alone. The big city of Campinas, where the cars usually sped by like they were playing Dodgems, was now almost empty of cars and pedestrians. Not even the motorcycles that traveled at break-neck speeds were out today. All was still and calm.

When I finally arrived at the airport, I was the first in line to take my luggage to the check-in. There were no people behind me. I searched for a place that served something to eat that would carry me over until the day's journey was done. I made my way to customs, and there was not one other person leaving Brazil. I walked quickly through the maze to make it to the officer at the booth. As an American, I was put right through. There was no one behind me and no one in front of me in the big auditorium that usually held thousands of people at any given time. I kept on my heavy black mask as I looked past duty-free fragrant perfume stores that had diminished to a ghost town without any hustle and bustle. I took some pictures; then I sat at my gate all alone for most of the evening until the plane would take off. A few gentlemen, probably Americans, were also taking the long night flight out of Brazil.

"Do not take your mask off for any reason, or you will be removed from this flight!" the steward said. The plane was nearly empty, and I had a whole aisle to myself, which meant I could probably grab some sleep.

When the food carts started to go around, the steward made another announcement. "Do not take your mask off, even to eat! You may pull up your mask to put the food in your mouth, but then you must pull it right back down again!"

I wasn't that hungry.

## CHAPTER 46
# The Last Breath

*"Let every thing that hath breath praise the Lord. Praise ye the Lord."*

Psalm 150:6

# New Franklin, Ohio
April 2021

"It's good to have you home," my mom, said. "Archie and Alyce have been waiting on you."

"It's good to be home."

"We have a bridal shower to go to, and we want to see Aunt Pat today!"

She had picked me up from the airport, and we chit-chatted on the way. I had been in quarantine for months in Brazil, and it felt good to be out and about. My daughter, Isa, was concerned that it was taking a long time for the vaccine to come to Brazil, so she arranged for me to get my first dose at a Walmart in Ohio the day after I arrived. I looked out the window of the familiar sights of Ohio. Lush, green trees along the highway and a Bob Evan's restaurant sign brought me back to familiarity. Arriving home, the smell of banana bread permeated my senses.

Archie and Alyce were two cute, cuddly cats: one a large white male and the other a small tortoise-colored female. When they were kittens, they were thought to be brother and sister. They sure did fight like a brother and sister, but they were extremely different in stature and color as they grew older. Archie was the affectionate one, and Alyce was a loner. She only ventured on your lap after she really knew you well or if it was cold and she wanted to sleep on a blanket. Archie hogged the food and chased Alyce around the house until she slinked under a chair, where his fat body failed to follow. In the middle of the night, Archie came into my bed, sleeping quietly at my feet and purring like an old-time furnace.

The next morning, I listened in to Cody's live prayer time for Gracious Daughters in the Netherlands. She gave a glorious Bible study filled with hope. Afterward, we left to pick up Aunt Polly and quickly made our way down the road to Aunt Pat's house. Inside her house, it was an unearthly calm as Aunt Pat lay in a hospital bed in the middle of the room. She looked extraordinarily thin, and it was clear her time was short.

"Jill's here," my mom said.

Aunt Pat then sat up in her bed. I went around to give her a hug. We had a time of laughter together as we heard each other's stories. For that moment, I forgot all about the pandemic, death, and suffering. We could laugh about things that usually weren't that funny. Aunt Polly talked about how spring was coming, and it would be time to plant the garden soon. Her daughter, Marsha, had been very ill recently. We decided to join hands and pray together. At the end, we declared that no matter what, God was always there; and God was always good.

"I love you, Aunt Pat," I said quietly when the others weren't around.

"You know that I love you, too, very much!"

Aunt Pat's last weeks were full ones with visits from her daughters and sons.

"When the tree out front blooms with its bright yellow flowers, then I will be ready to go to Heaven."

The tree without a name had been transplanted from West Virginia from Vernon's family farm. Usually, around May, it strutted its exquisite golden colors and stood apart from all the other trees that were plain green. As surely as the day it bloomed, Aunt Pat took her last breath on earth and went to live in Heaven with Jesus, Whom she had loved and served all her life.

# Delicious Banana Bread
## by Judy Baughman

- ½ cup shortening
- 1 cup sugar
- 2 eggs
- 3 mashed bananas
- ½ cup ground walnuts (optional)
- 2 cups flour
- ½ tsp. soda
- ½ tsp. salt
- ½ tsp. baking powder

## Directions:

1. Preheat oven to 350 degrees F. Grease one loaf pan, and then add 1 teaspoon of sifted flour on the bottom.
2. Cream shortening and sugar by hand or with a mixer.
3. Add eggs, the mashed bananas, and remaining ingredients.
4. Bake at 350 degrees F for 45 to 60 minutes. When the smell fills the kitchen and a toothpick inserted comes out clean, then it is done. Wait 15 minutes for it to cool before slicing.

CHAPTER 47

## A Double Portion

*"And the LORD turned the captivity of Job, when he prayed for his friends: also the LORD gave Job twice as much as he had before."*

Job 42:10

### Holambra
2021

"Papa, you need a new dog!" Jeremy said. He was on a visit from Texas to Brazil. "Look at Maxima; she is so lonely."

Maxima was a regal white bulldog named for Queen Maxima of the Netherlands. Contrary to the beautiful Dutch queen, there were times that she liked to roll around in the mud outside, and then she resembled a pig as she waddled around the house.

"I don't know, son. We said we wouldn't get another dog!" Paul said.

"Well, it never hurts to just look," I said.

"Let's go!" said Henrique.

The four of us set off to Sorocaba, a city located about an hour and a half away, where we would visit a kennel of Belgium shepherds—the Groenendael. It was a long drive but a welcome trip after being cooped up all month in quarantine.

We finally arrived at the home and were greeted by a woman with multiple tiny, black fluffs wriggling around on the tiled floor.

"Oh, my goodness," I said as I breathed in the sweetness of the little puppies. They were like little, furry bear cubs with tiny, black dot eyes. One rested in Jeremy's arms, and one rested in Paul's arms.

"I like these two, but which one should we get?"

One of the puppies was thick around the belly, and the other puppy was a little more petite with finer features.

"Why don't we get both?" I suggested.

"Can we?" asked Paul. He lifted his head in surprise, the joy shining from his eyes.

"Why not?" I asked. "They will be a comfort to one another."

We named them Gracie and Maggie. They came to the van Opstal home looking like little bear cubs; but as they continued to grow bigger and bigger, they resembled black wolves and became very active, loyal dogs. Paul called them his big black monsters at times, and they made lots of messes. At times, Maxima loved her two new sisters; and at times, she barely tolerated the two shepherds.

## Lar Feliz, Jaguariúna
April 2021

"Just dig a little deeper," said Sidnei. "I know there is something down there." The large shovel of the equipment finally stopped as a spring of clean water gurgled and bubbled to the surface.

"We have water!"

"That will make a big difference in paying the water bill," said Paul.

Through the intuition of Sidnei, the men found an underground spring on the Lar Feliz land near the community center. The spring of clean and living water was located smack dab in between the first and second farms owned by Lar Feliz.

The first farm, which was originally used for work teams, was now rented out to a men's recuperation home. Many men were coming through as the drug problem in Brazilian society continued to grow. Johan Toet, our Dutch friend, made monthly visits to the home and led many men to give their lives to Jesus. Soon after they made decisions, they were baptized and became regular members of our church. A twenty-minute walk down the road led to the children's homes, Lar Feliz.

"There should be plenty of water for all!" said Sidnei.

Even though we lost our building where we had originally planted the church, the Lord gave us double for what we had before: land, water, a parking lot, new members, and a brand-new building! Ever since we opened the doors of our new building, it was full. The days of an empty building with expensive rent were behind us now.

CHAPTER 48

# A Beautiful Bride

*"And I John saw the holy city, new Jerusalem, coming down from God out of heaven, prepared as a bride adorned for her husband."*

Revelation 21:2

## Lar Féliz Community Center
2021

The gentle worship music began, and the people filed in to take a seat at their new church building. Henrique had made sure that the sound equipment was of the best quality available, and it showed. Every detail had been thought through: the hanging lamps at the sides that gave a cozy feeling and the chocolate brown wall at the front of the sanctuary—an accent color that drew the eye to the band and the preacher. Everything was pretty much ready; and every seat in the church was full, all eyes fixed forward with hands raised in worship and prayer.

Only a week earlier, the men from the rehab home had heard about Jesus from Johan and Brenda and their group of *Nederlanders*. After listening to their testimonies and the Word of God, the men had received Jesus as their Lord and were baptized. They were new creations. The old had passed away, and the new had come.[24]

---
24  2 Corinthians 5:17

Across the aisle, was a large group of children, quietly sitting in small groupings with brothers and sisters and monitors from the home. The girls were dressed in flowery dresses, and the boys were in their best jeans and tennis shoes. They had all walked to church from their home at Lar Feliz under the clear, night sky that was filled with stars.

"Oi, Pastor Paul!" They all waved "hello" as Paul made his way to the pulpit. He opened the service with a word of praise to the Lord for all that He brought us through.

A familiar melody of praise filled the church as Camily, the young leader of the dance, began to interpret the words of the song through creative movement. Gislaine, a young woman sitting in the back with her small daughter, Manu, was stirred and revived. She would later join the church and serve in many ways.

There were families who came and joined from Mogi Mirim, Jaguariúna, Holambra, and even Pedreira. All worshipped in one room together to the soft, tender music of the band. After the last song was sung, Keila, the sister of Kaira, walked with bowed head to the back of the church and up the circular stairs that led to the children's classrooms. A mob of little children followed closely behind her, eager for their lesson from the Bible. Keila was a soft-spoken girl, and she loved the children who came to church. Feeling this love, the children behaved and listened with open hearts, eager to return to church every week.

## CHAPTER 49
# A Ready Bride

*"And the Spirit and the bride say, 'Come.' And let him that heareth say, 'Come.' And let him that is athirst come. And whosoever will, let him take the water of life freely."*

Revelation 22:17

## Ishabela
September 11, 2021

It was springtime in Brazil. The winter had passed, and white and purple orchids were in bloom in the garden. The temperature outside was perfect—not too hot and not too cold. As we drove down the highway, we arrived at the ferry that would take us to the island. Isa had flown in from Texas, and the three of us were going to a wedding that day—the long-awaited wedding of Franklin and Petra.

Paul was the translator, so we arrived at the church one hour earlier than the rest. The grand windows of the church had a view of the sea; and the old, dark, wood pillars of the hall matched the natural color of the sanctuary. Rustic white shutters trimmed the large windows against the light brick walls. White chrysanthemums in baskets were placed on the floor at the end of each aisle, and the sound men were setting up the last details. Paul chatted with the pastor, who was originally from Germany but married a beautiful woman from Brazil.

The guests started to flow into the grand hall, and the musicians started to play in beautiful tones. Families and singles came in and sat in their seats; and it was spread around that for the first time that anyone had known her, Petra was running late. This was her special day that would only come around once in her life, and she could take her time at the hairdresser!

The music continued, and the signal was given by the pastor for everyone to stand. The congregation gently stood, and every eye was fixed toward the back of the church. Petra came walking in, her arm linked with her Dutch father. Her long blonde hair was braided into a circle that flowed down her back. Her white dress with the lacy white bodice gave her a royal appearance.

Franklin, who stood at the front, was noticeably moved; and his smile radiated over his entire face. His mother in the front row clapped her hand over her mouth in surprise as Petra solemnly passed. Franklin's words were heard by those of us in the front row.

"You are beautiful!"

CHAPTER 50

# Back to the Beginning

*"To every thing there is a season, and a time to every purpose under the heaven: a time to be born, and a time to die; a time to plant, and a time to pluck up that which is planted."*

Ecclesiastes 3:1-2

There is a time for everything. Brazil had gone through hardships and grief during the pandemic with the loss of lives in the tens of thousands. The economy had been shaken, but now it was the time to sing and to start again. It was time to build again and put to rest the pain that we had gone through. God was faithful through it all. Hand in hand, God's people would dream and hope for a new day and a future that was prosperous and bright.

During the time that we were first living in Brazil, together with our Brazilian staff and volunteers, we were able to build a happy home for children brick by brick and mortared with prayer upon prayer. Lar Feliz was growing in number again, and the Lord sent provision to us from many people throughout Brazil and the world. Churches in Holambra began to work closer together for the common goal of shining the bright light of Jesus. All that we had dreamed of was close to conception.

At church in Brazil, there is a song that we sing that talks about Jesus being our Home. Wherever I go, I am at home because Jesus is always with me.

## Finding a Happy Home

*Let me tell you a story*
*About a young mother*
*Who moved to a new place.*
*She lived with a new people,*
*Who didn't speak her language.*
*She was afraid*
*Most of the time.*
*Until one day,*
*Because of the love of Jesus,*
*She became brave enough*
*To love with a selfless heart.*
*Then, everything*
*That she desired*
*Came to her in time.*
*As she helped the poor,*
*She became rich.*
*When she found a home*
*For the lost,*
*She found one, too.*

*And she planted*
*A garden with exotic flowers*
*Where many birds nested*
*And cats came to play.*
*Her own children grew;*
*And moving on,*
*They became the toast of Texas.*
*Still, she stayed with her man,*
*In the wild land of Brazil.*
*And that girl is me!*

# Author Biography

Jill van Opstal-Popa is an ordinary woman who knows an extraordinary God. She is the wife of Paul and mother to three grown children. Though she is originally from Akron, Ohio, she has been involved with missions for nearly thirty-four years. She first served at YWAM Amsterdam where she met her husband, Paul. For the past twenty-two years they have served together in Brazil where they founded Lar Feliz, or "Happy Home," By God's grace, she has been able to help over 2,500 children through this thriving ministry. They also planted a flourishing church called *Comunidade Nove e Livre*. She lives to proclaim the matchless grace and love that is found in Jesus Christ; to Him be all the glory.

Ambassador International's mission is to magnify the Lord Jesus Christ and promote His Gospel through the written word.

We believe through the publication of Christian literature, Jesus Christ and His Word will be exalted, believers will be strengthened in their walk with Him, and the lost will be directed to Jesus Christ as the only way of salvation.

For more information about
AMBASSADOR INTERNATIONAL
please visit:

www.ambassador-international.com
@AmbassadorIntl
www.facebook.com/AmbassadorIntl

*Thank you for reading this book!*

*You make it possible for us to fulfill our mission, and we are grateful for your partnership.*

*To help further our mission, please consider leaving us a review on your social media, favorite retailer's website, Goodreads or Bookbub, or our website, and check out some of our other books on the next page!*

# More from Ambassador International

In *#NoFilter: Unmasking the Woman God Created You to Be*, Jodi Hendricks helps you challenge the filters that have enslaved you, discover the calling to which you've been called, and to bask in the truth that as creatures of the Creator Himself, you need no filter. The Almighty Who created you has had a plan and a purpose for you since you were knit together in your mother's womb, and He has called you to walk in a manner worthy of this calling.

*Your Story Isn't Over Yet* is a true story of how the sovereignty of God worked through the horrors of domestic violence, sexual assault, abortion, and trauma to ultimately show His unconditional love. Follow Grace's path of pain, loss, and perseverance to a pandemic love story and the joy that can be found only in Jesus.

Throughout her years serving alongside her husband, who pastored Southside Baptist Church (now Fellowship Greenville) in Greenville, South Carolina, for over thirty years, Elizabeth Rice Handford has had the opportunity to touch many lives with her daily devotionals. In her new devotional, *Fullness of Joy*, take a dive into one hundred of Libby's devotionals, compiled from a look back through her writings and life experiences.

www.ingramcontent.com/pod-product-compliance
Lightning Source LLC
Chambersburg PA
CBHW060459090426
42735CB00011B/2045